Masterpieces of

Van Dyck

(1907)

ISBN-13 : 978-1512310658

ISBN-10 : 1512310654

Notice

This documentary study use historic, archived documents.

Because of this, some pages may look blurry or low quality.

Still are included in this book because they have

high value from critical, documentary, historical,

informative and journalistic point of view .

Dtp
and
visual art

Iacob Adrian

THE

MASTERPIECES

OF

VAN DYCK

(1599-1641)

*Sixty reproductions of photographs from the original paintings
by F. Hanfstaengl, affording examples of the different
characteristics of the Artist's work*

Author statement

This is a series of art books .

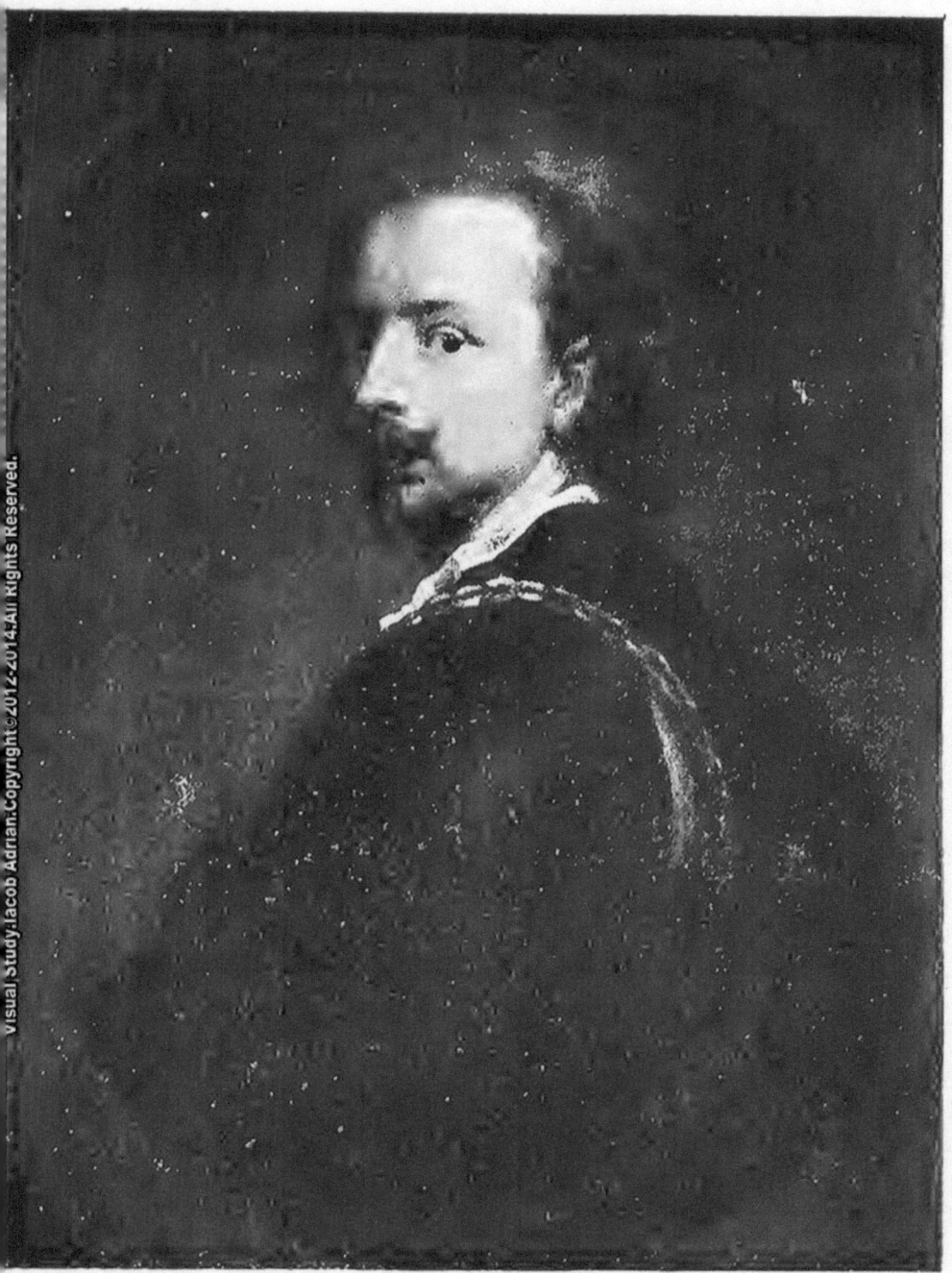

PORTRAIT OF HIMSELF PORTRAIT DE L'ARTISTE
(*Uffizi, Florence*) (*Galerie des Uffizi, Florence*)

SELBSTBILDNIS
(*Florenz, Uffizien*)
F. Hanfstaengl, Photo.

This little Book conveys the greetings of

....

to

....

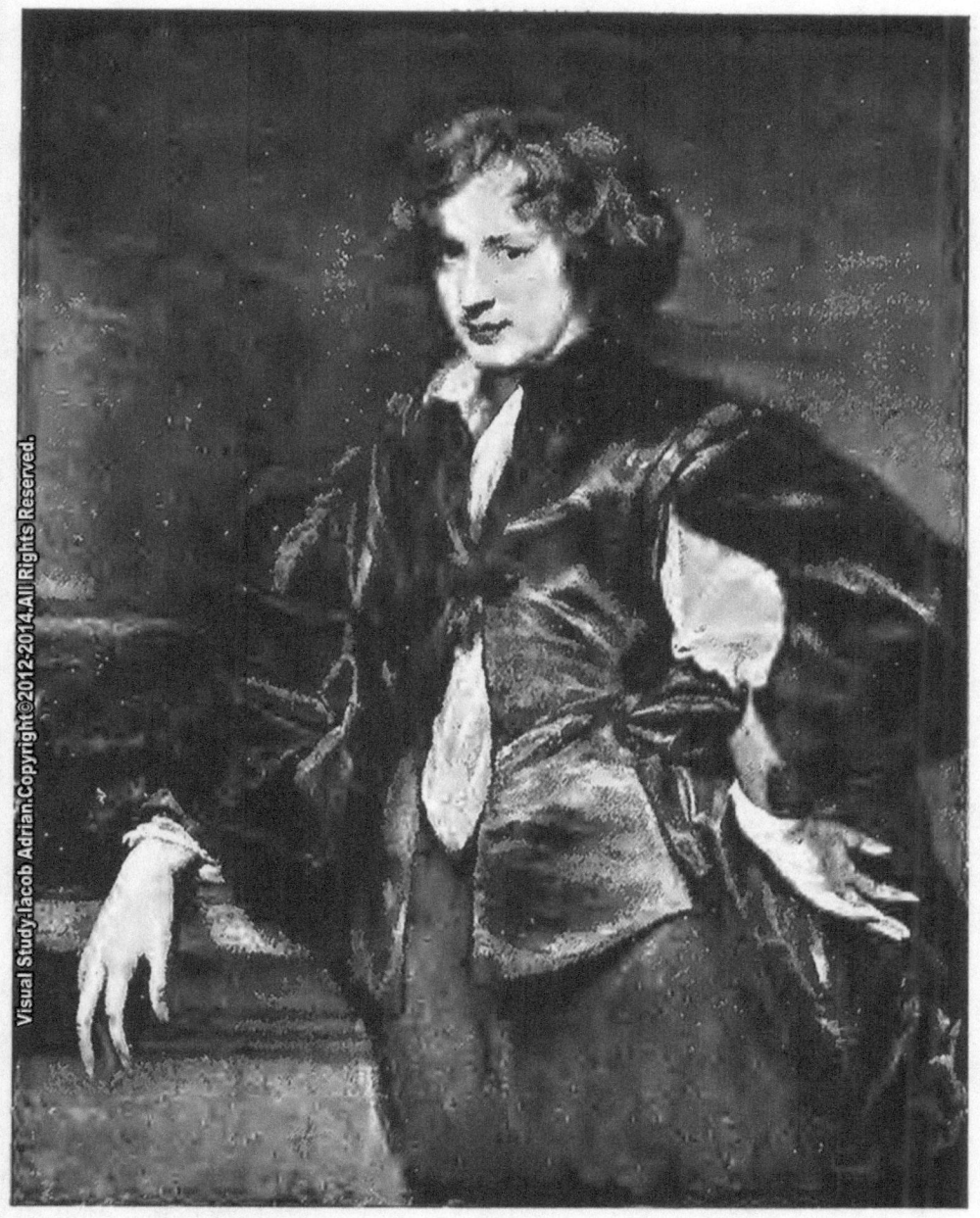

PORTRAIT OF HIMSELF IN HIS YOUTH
(*The Hermitage, St. Petersburg*)

PORTRAIT DE L'ARTISTE, ENCORE JEUNE
(*L'Ermitage, Saint-Pétersbourg*)

SELBSTBILDNIS IN JUNGEN JAHREN
(*Petersburg, Eremitage*)
F. Hanfstaengl, Photo.

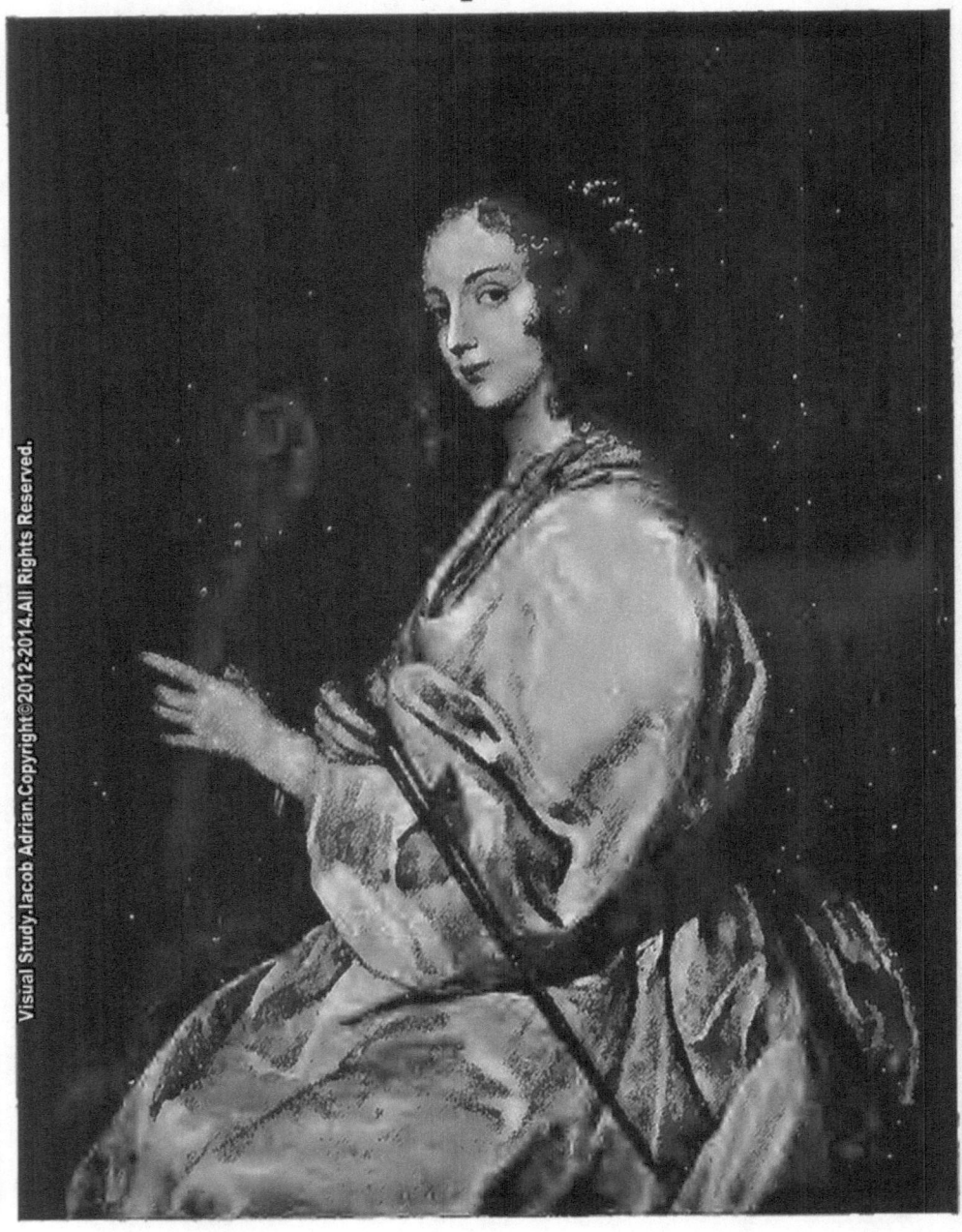

THE ARTIST'S WIFE
(*Pinakothek, Munich*)

LA FEMME DE L'ARTISTE
(*Pinacothèque, Munich*)

DIE FRAU DES MEISTERS
(*München, Pinakothek*)
F. Hanfstaengl, Photo.

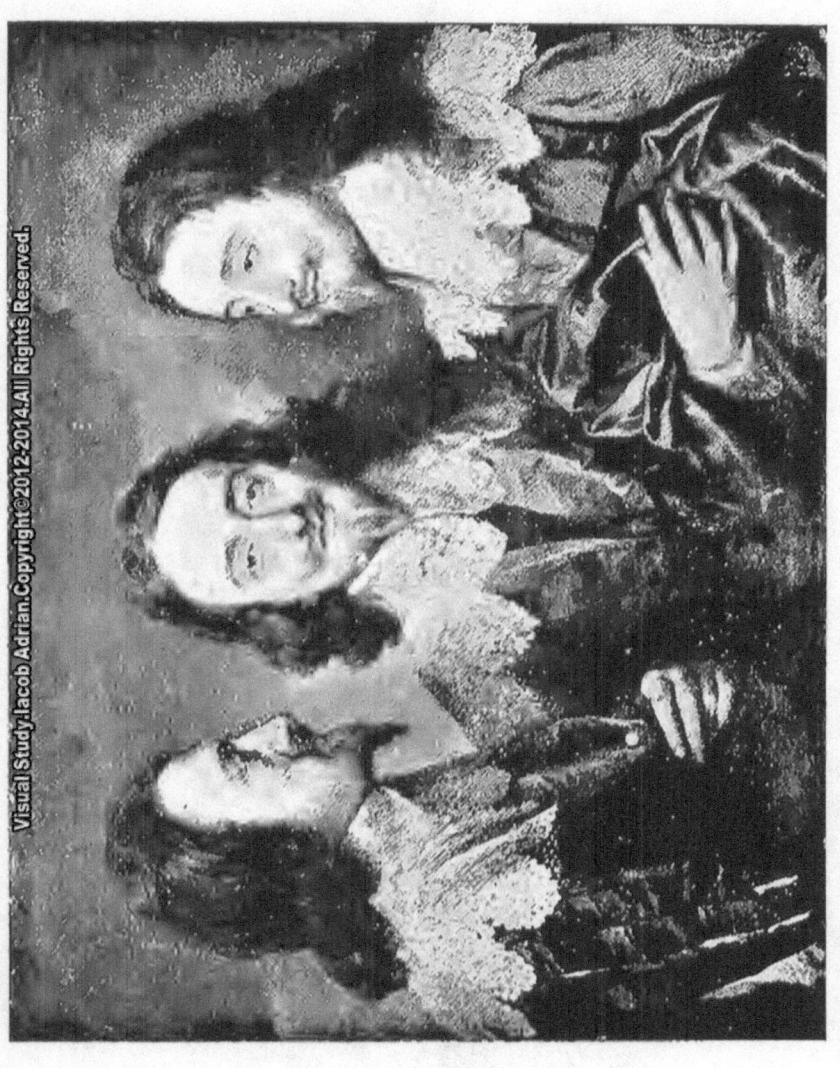

CHARLES I.
(*Windsor Castle*)

CHARLES Ier
(*Galerie royale, Windsor*)

KARL I. KÖNIG VON ENGLAND
(*Windsor, Kgl. Schloss*)   *F. Hanfstaengl, Photo.*

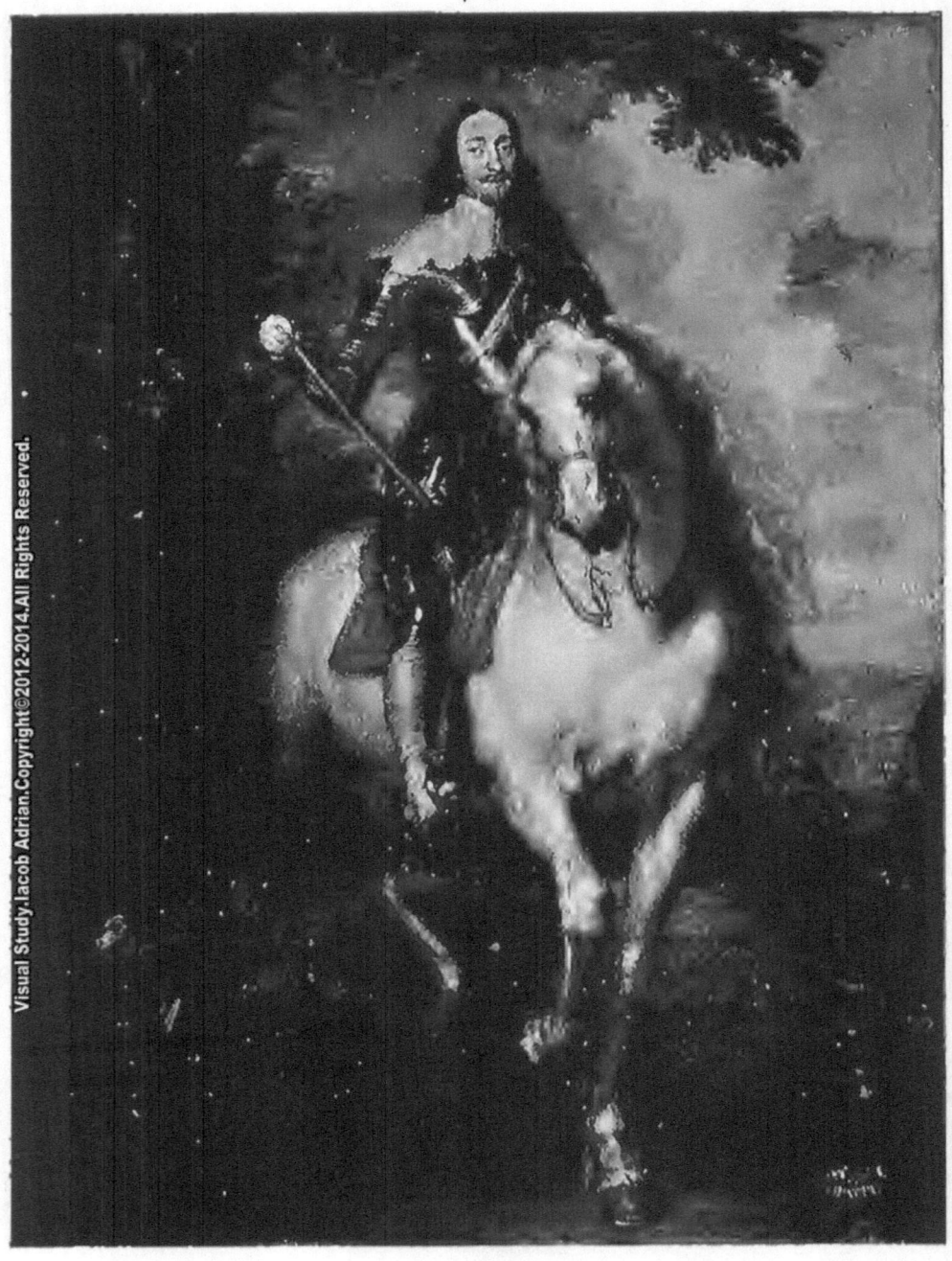

EQUESTRIAN PORTRAIT OF CHARLES I.   CHARLES IER À CHEVAL
(*Prado, Madrid*)   (*Prado, Madrid*)
EIN REITERBILDNIS VON KARL I., KÖNIG VON ENGLAND
(*Madrid, Prado*)
F. Hanfstaengl, Photo.

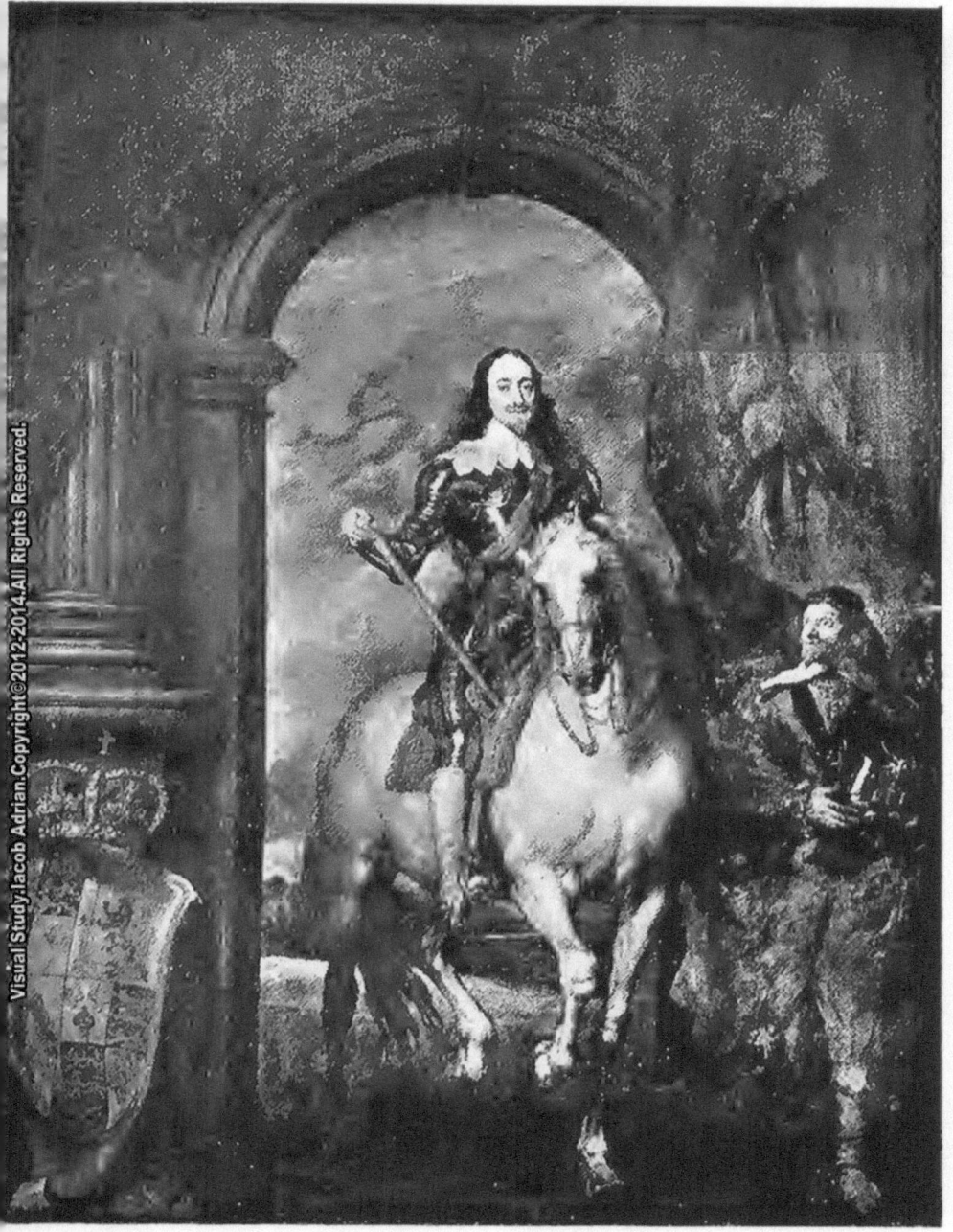

EQUESTRIAN PORTRAIT OF CHARLES I.   CHARLES IER À CHEVAL
(*Windsor Castle*)   (*Galerie royale, Windsor*)
EIN REITERBILDNIS VON KARL I., KÖNIG VON ENGLAND
(*Windsor, Kgl. Schloss*)
F. Hanfstaengl, Photo.

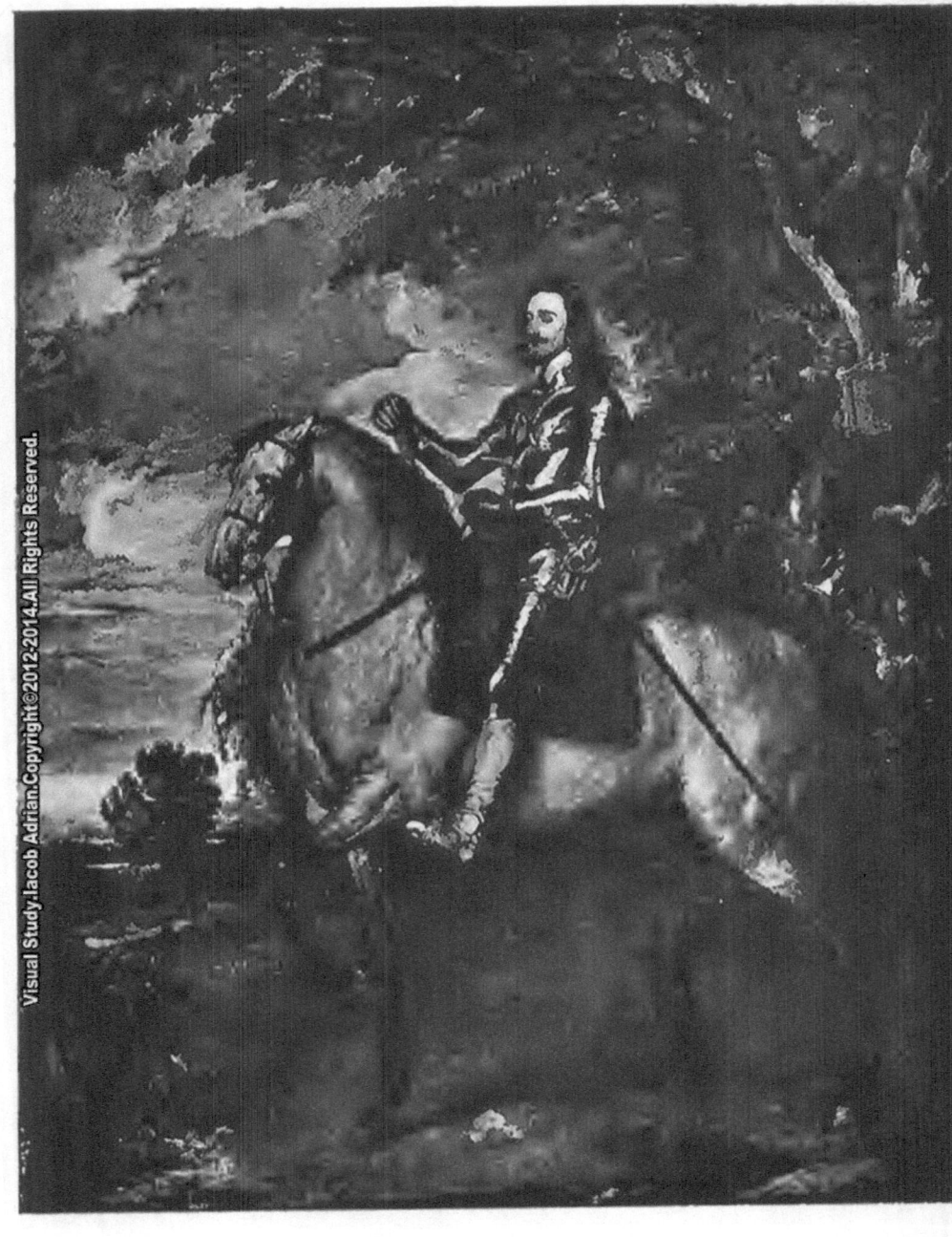

EQUESTRIAN PORTRAIT OF CHARLES I.   CHARLES IᴇR À CHEVAL
(National Gallery, London)   *(Galerie nationale, Londres)*
EIN REITERBILDNIS VON KARL I., KÖNIG VON ENGLAND
(London, Nationalgalerie)
F. Hanfstaengl, Photo.

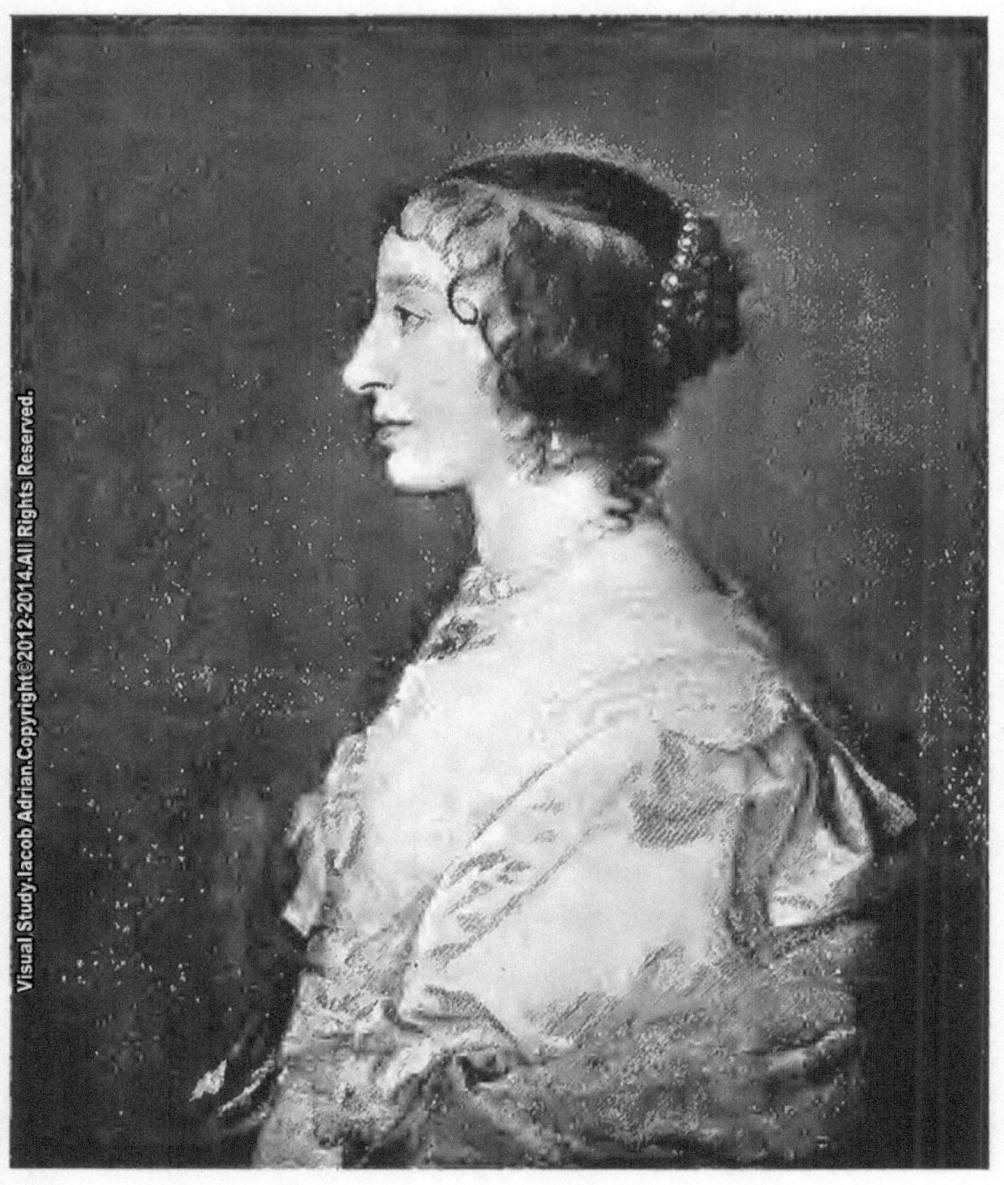

QUEEN HENRIETTA   HENRIETTE-MARIE, DE PROFIL
(*Windsor Castle*)   (*Galerie royale, Windsor*)
HENRIETTA MARIA, GEMAHLIN KARLS I.
(*Windsor, Kgl. Schloss*)
F. Hanfstaengl, Photo.

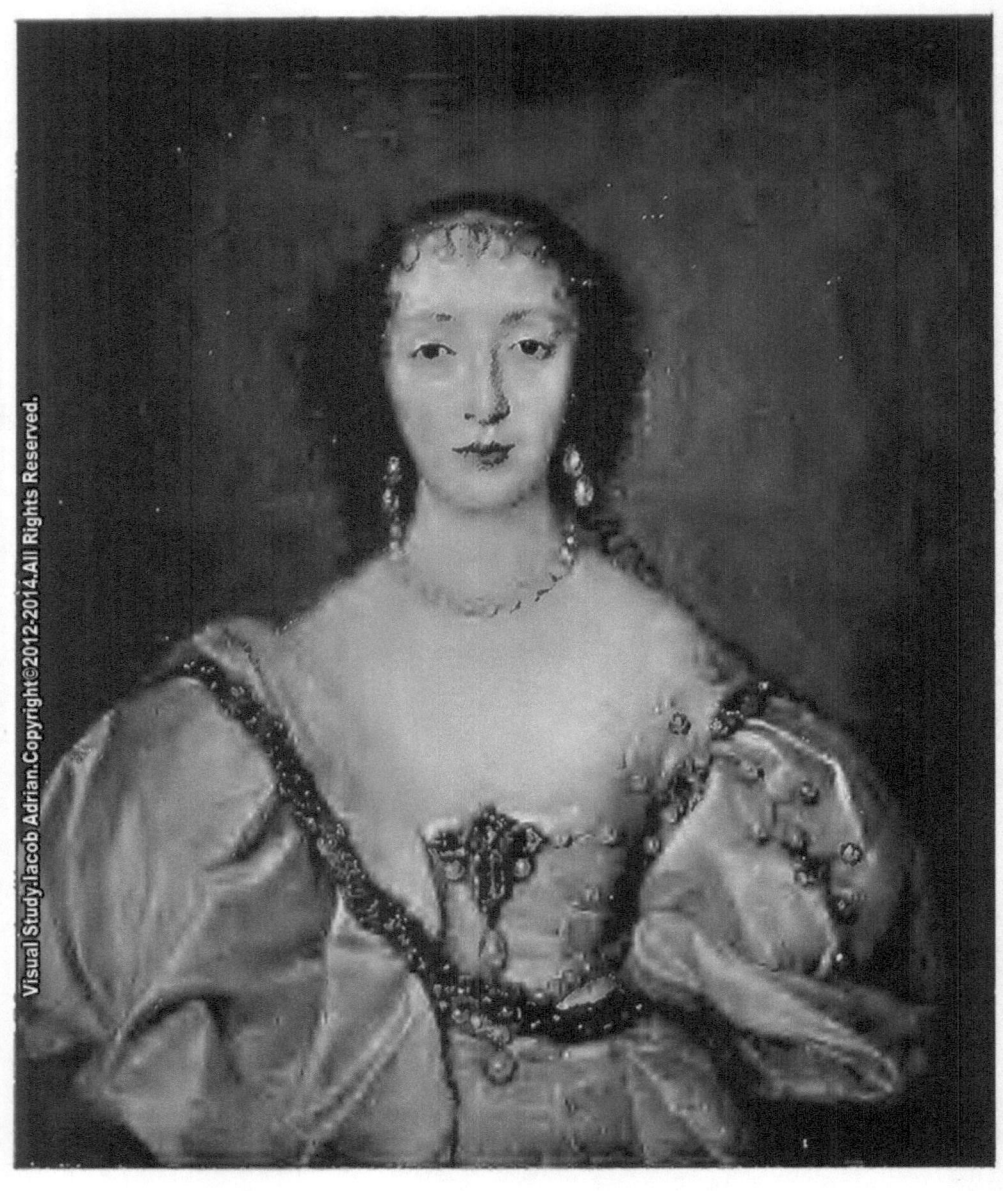

QUEEN HENRIETTA   HENRIETTE-MARIE, DE PROFIL
(Windsor Castle)   *(Galerie royale, Windsor)*
HENRIETTA MARIA, GEMAHLIN KARLS I.
(Windsor, Kgl. Schloss)
F. Hanfstaengl, Photo.

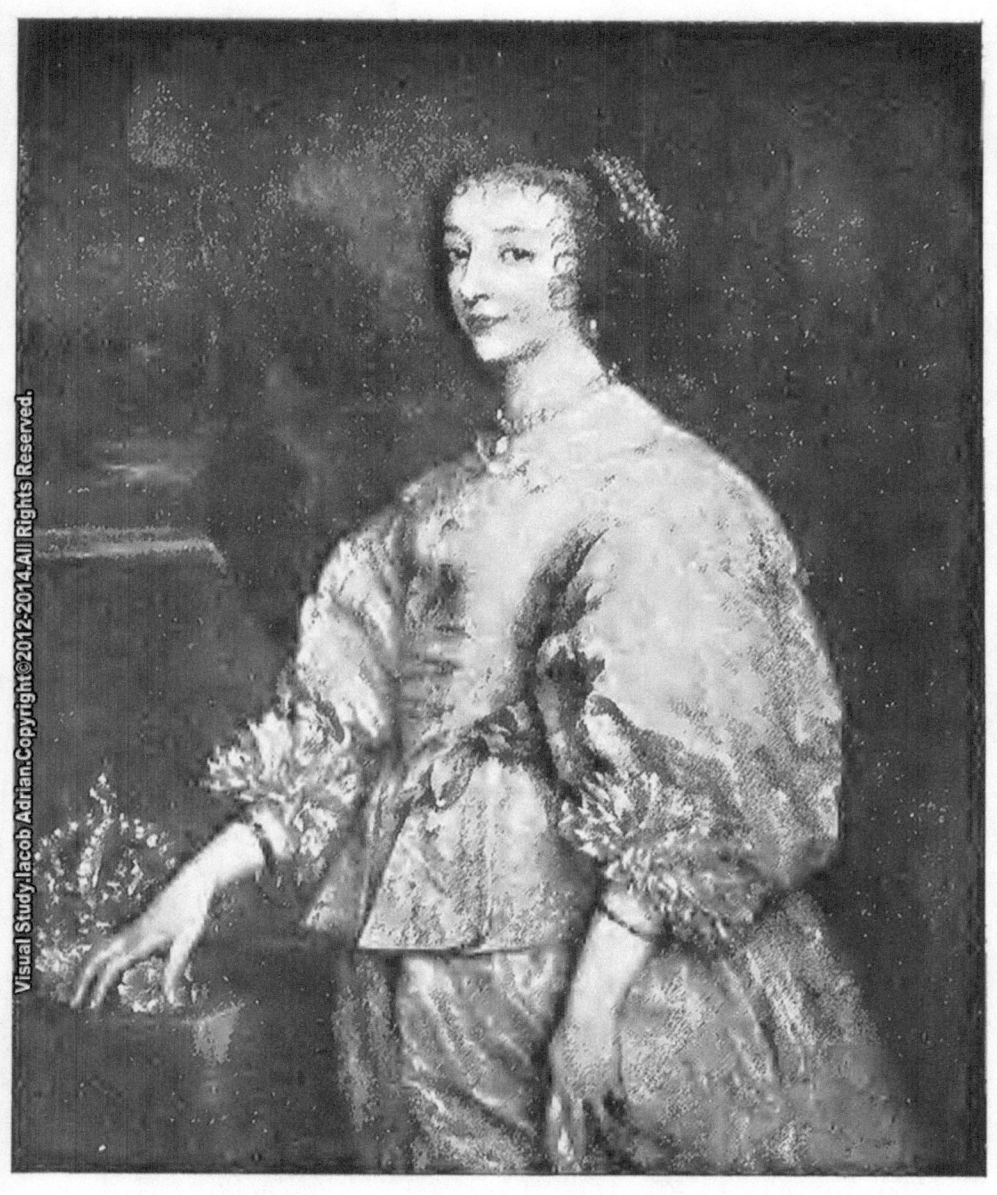

QUEEN HENRIETTA   HENRIETTE-MARIE, DE FACE
(*Windsor Castle*)   (*Galerie royale, Windsor*)
HENRIETTA MARIA, GEMAHLIN KARLS I.
(*Windsor, Kgl. Schloss*)
F. Hanfstaengl, Photo.

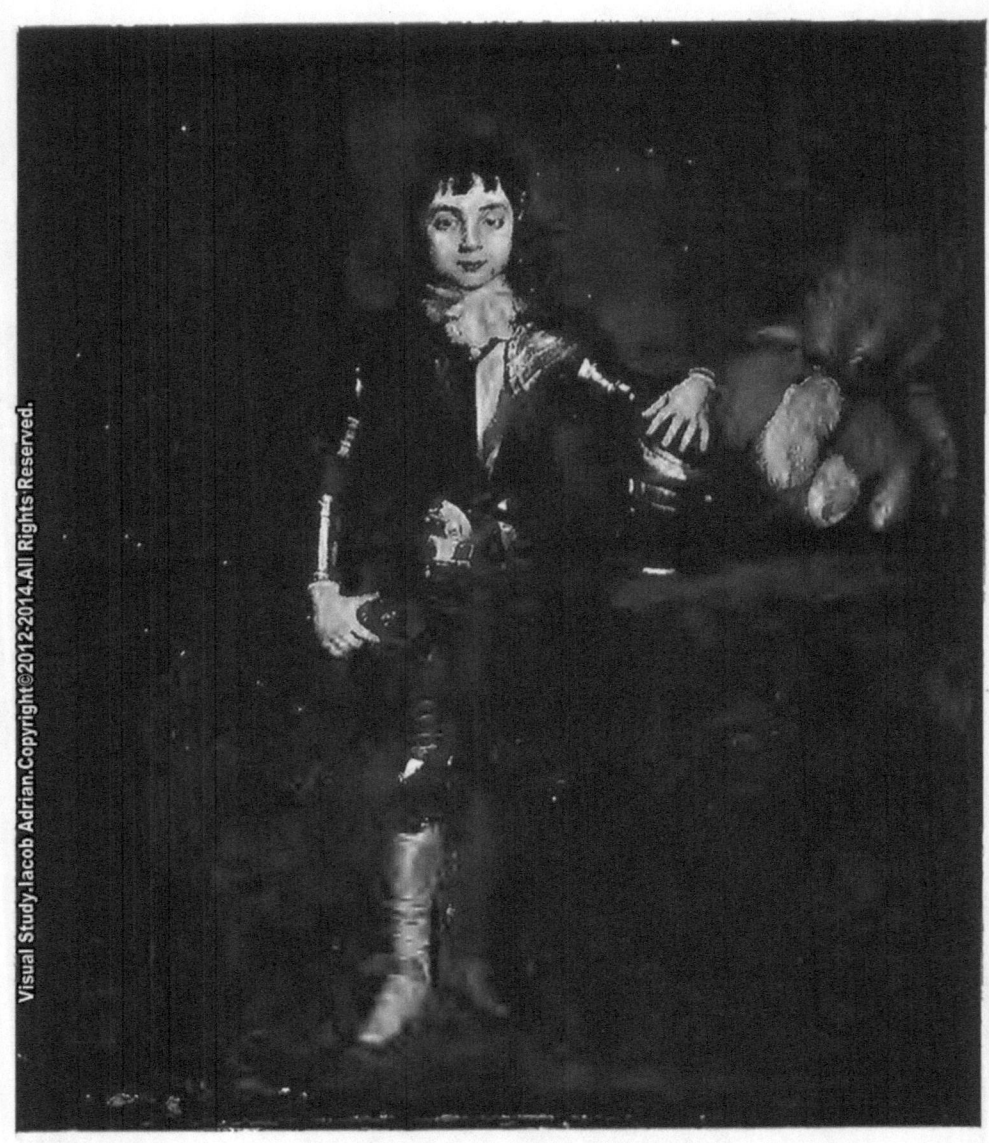

PRINCE CHARLES (CHARLES II.),   CHARLES II.
ELDEST SON OF CHARLES I.   VÊTU D'UNE ARMURE
(Windsor Castle)   *(Galerie royale, Windsor)*
PRINZ KARL (KARL II.), ÄLTESTER SOHN KÖNIGS KARL I.
(Windsor, Kgl. Schloss)
F. Hanfstaengl, Photo.

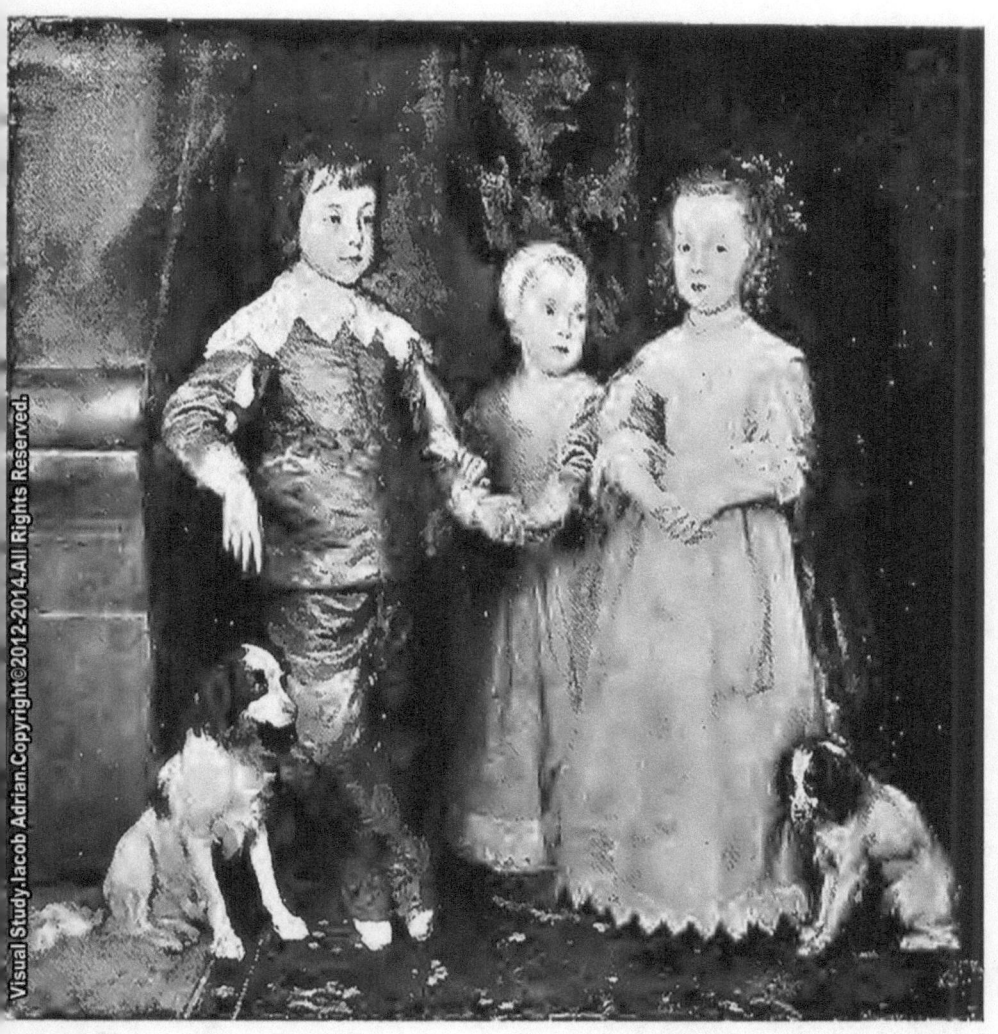

CHARLES, PRINCE OF WALES;   ENFANTS DE CHARLES IER, LE PRINCE
JAMES, DUKE OF YORK,   DE GALLES, LA PRINCESSE MARIE
AND PRINCESS MARY   ET LE DUC D'YORK
(*Windsor Castle*)   (*Galerie royale, Windsor*)
KARL, PRINZ VON WALES; JAMES, HERZOG VON YORK,
UND PRINZESSIN MARY
(*Windsor, Kgl. Schloss*)
F. Hanfstaengl, Photo.

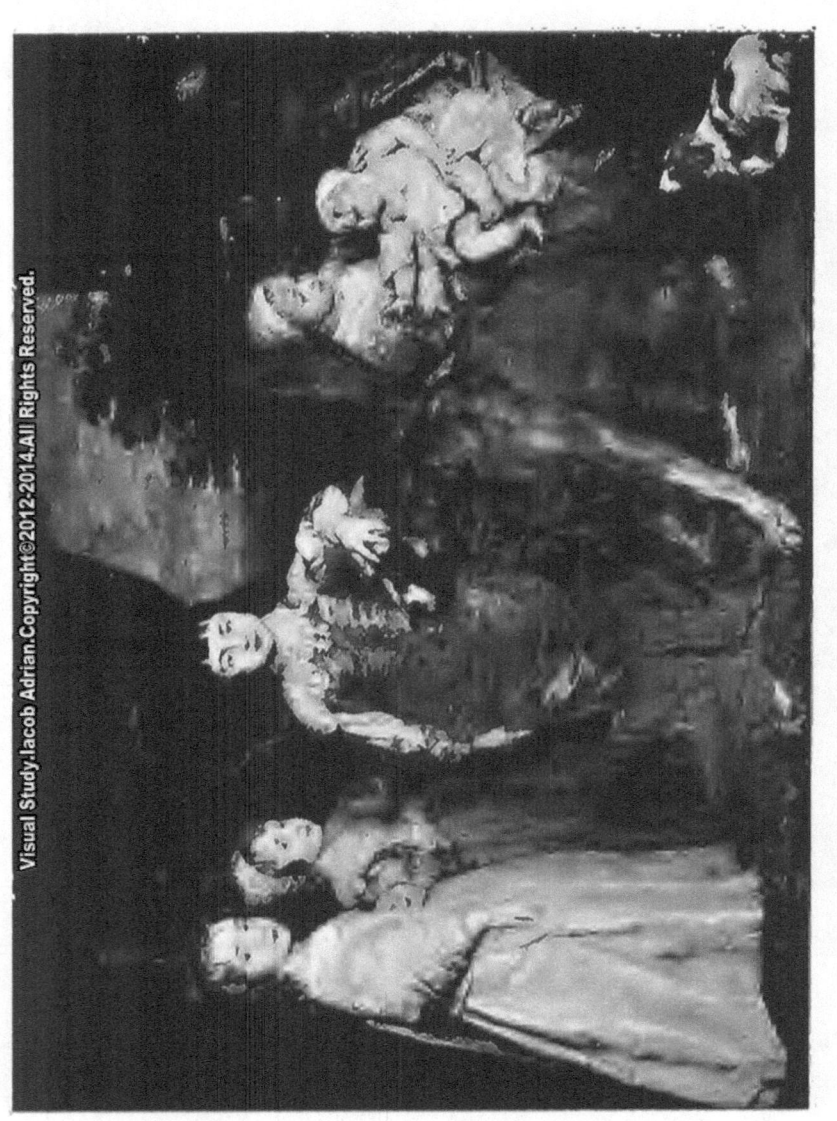

THE CHILDREN OF CHARLES I.   LES ENFANTS DE CHARLES IER
(*Windsor Castle*)   (*Galerie royale, Windsor*)
KINDER KARLS I.
(*Windsor, Kgl. Schloss*)
F. Hanfstaengl, Photo.

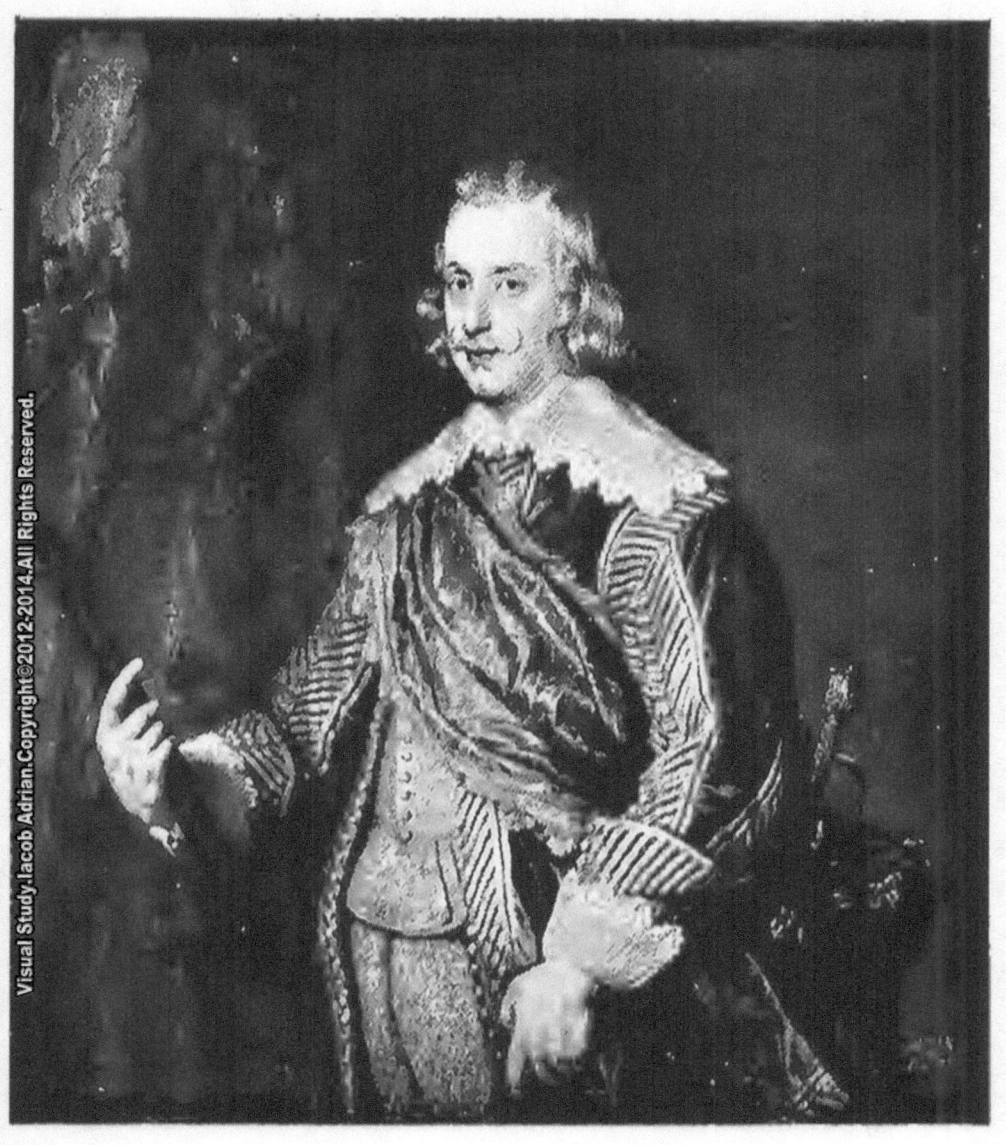

DON FERDINAND OF AUSTRIA   DON FERDINAND D'AUTRICHE
(*Prado, Madrid*)   (*Prado, Madrid*)
DON FERDINAND VON ÖSTERREICH
(*Madrid, Prado*)
F. Hanfstaengl, Photo.

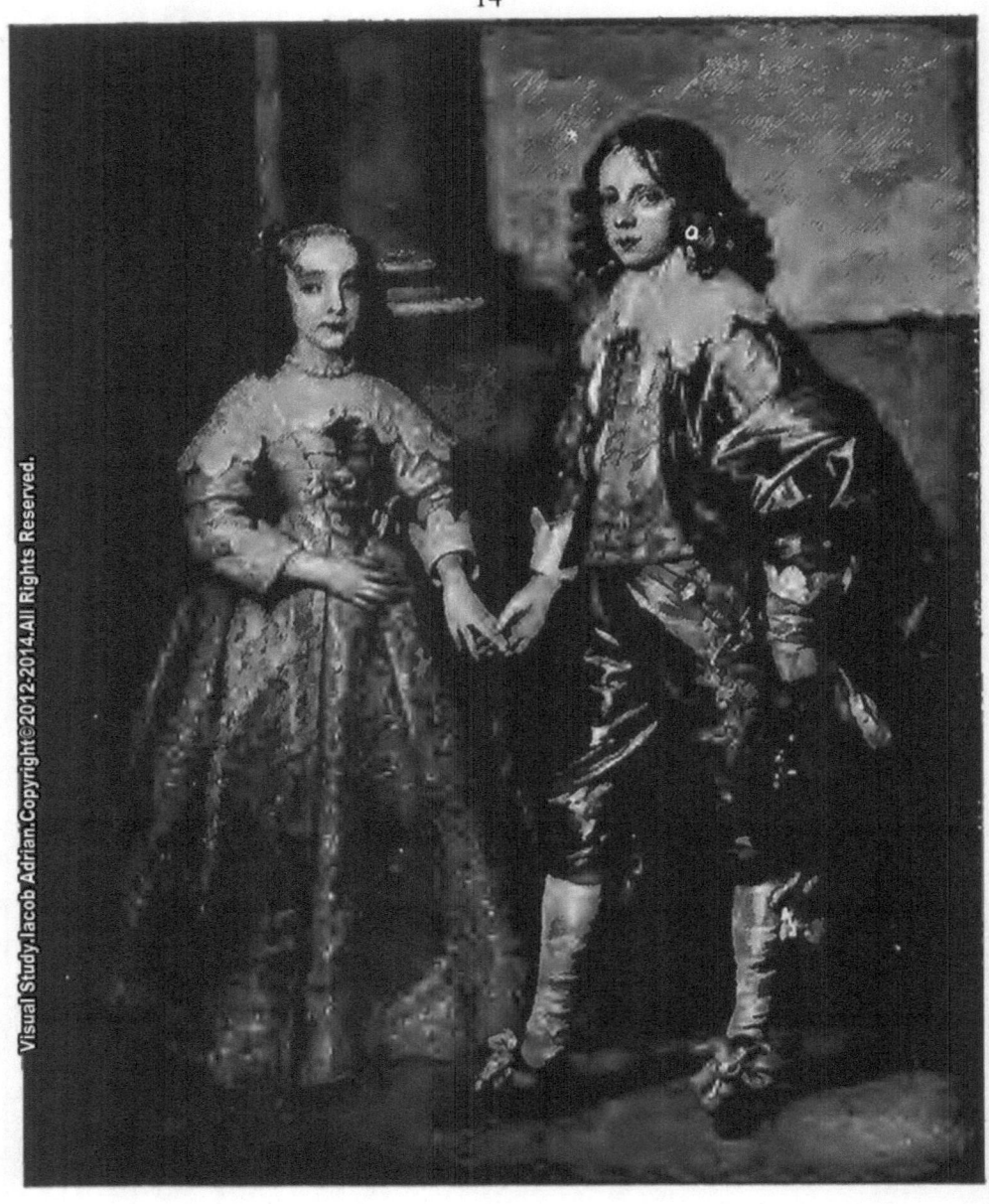

WILLIAM II. OF ORANGE AND HIS BRIDE,　LA PRINCESSE MARIE
MARIA HENRIETTA,　　　　AVEC SON FIANCÉ
DAUGHTER OF CHARLES I.　　　GUILLAUME II.
(Royal Museum, Amsterdam)　*(Musée royal, Amsterdam)*
WILHELM II. VON ORANIEN UND SEINE BRAUT,
MARIA HENRIETTA, TOCHTER KARLS I.
(Amsterdam, Kgl. Museum)
F. Hanfstaengl, Photo.

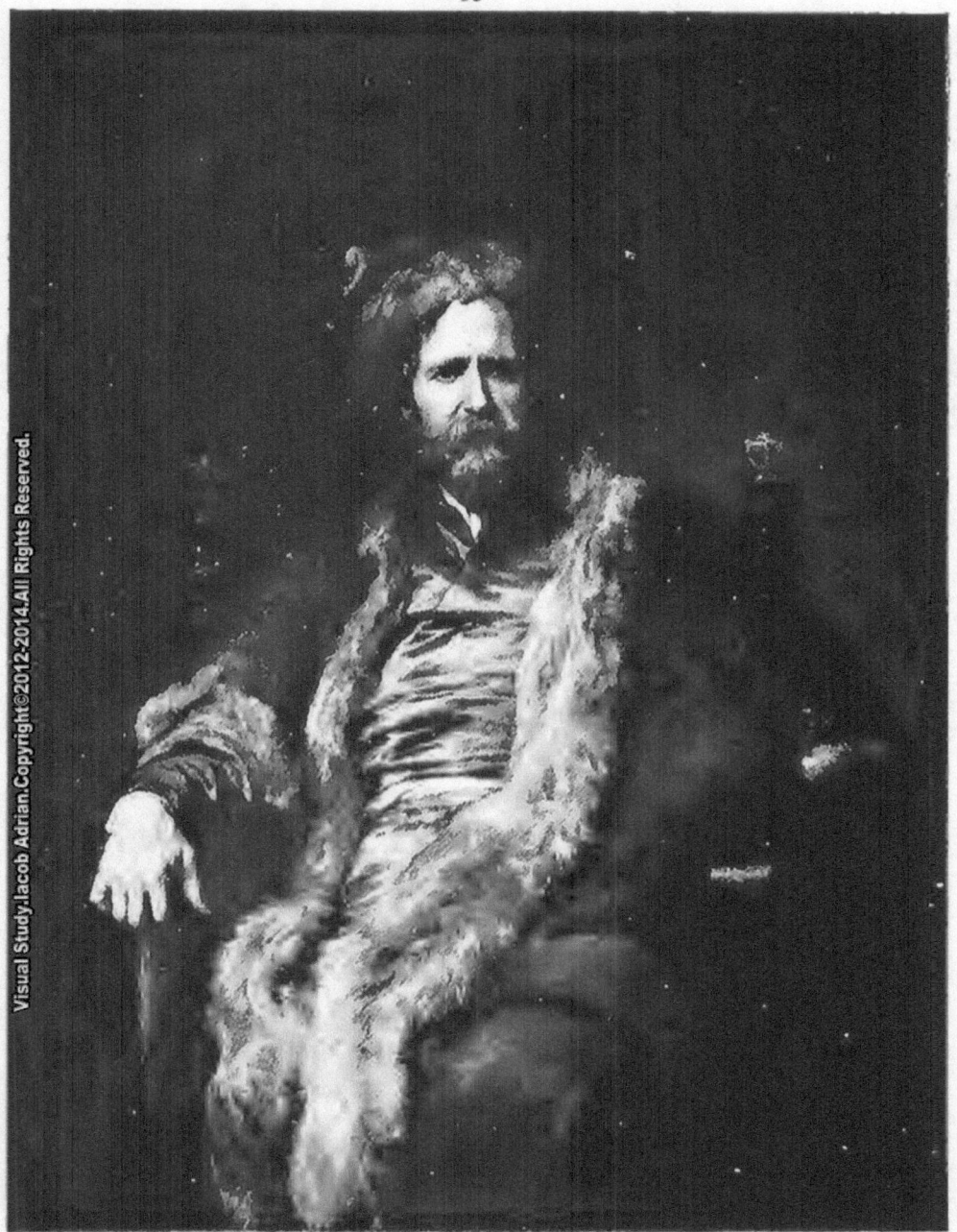

DAVID RYCKAERT
(*Prado, Madrid*)

DAVID RYCKAERT
(*Prado, Madrid*)

DAVID RYCKAERT
(*Madrid, Prado*)
F. Hanfstaengl, Photo.

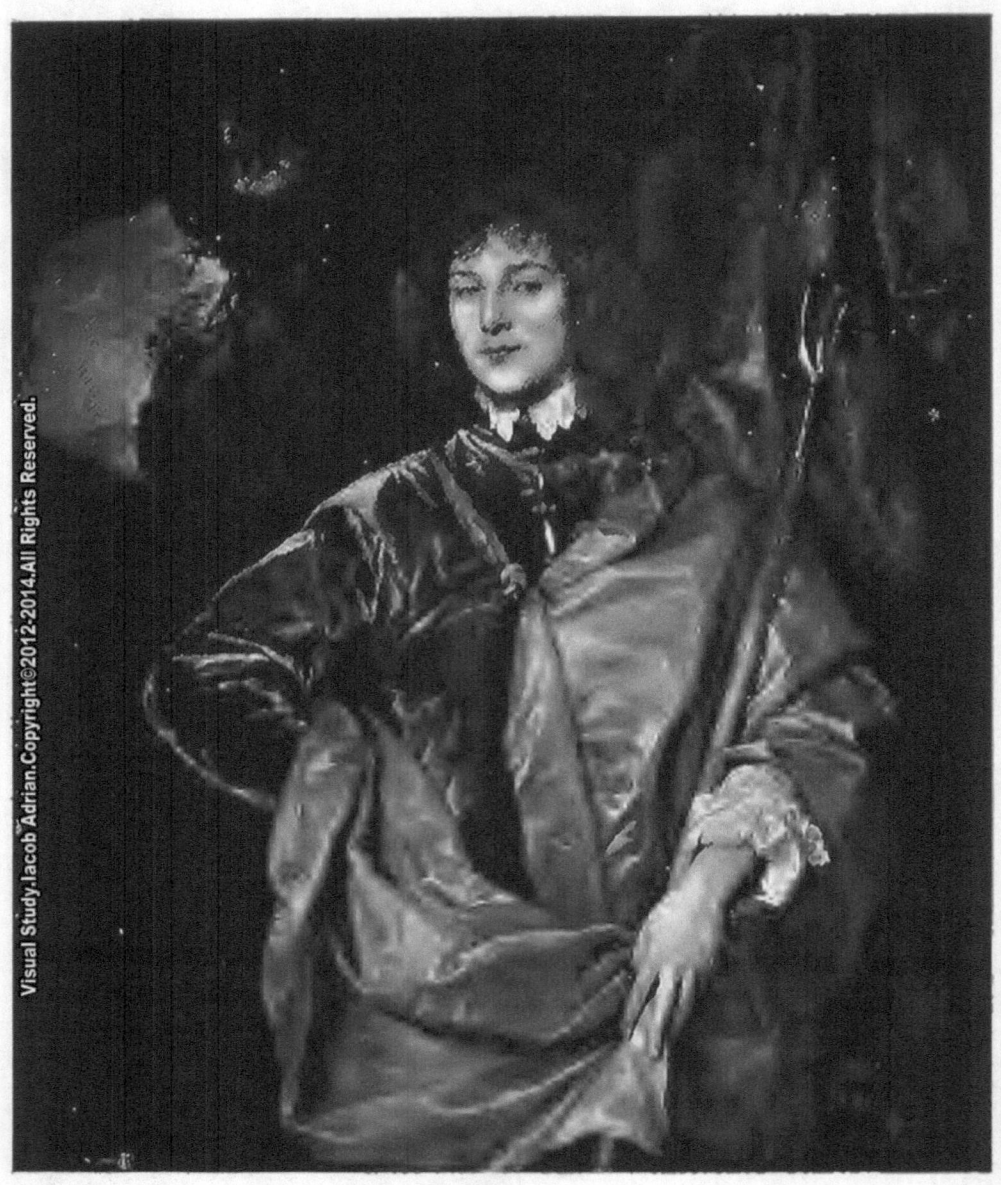

PHILIP, LORD WHARTON   PHILIPPE, LORD WHARTON
(The Hermitage, St. Petersburg)   *(L'Ermitage, Saint-Pétersbourg)*
PHILIP, LORD WHARTON
(Petersburg, Eremitage)
F. Hanfstaengl, Photo.

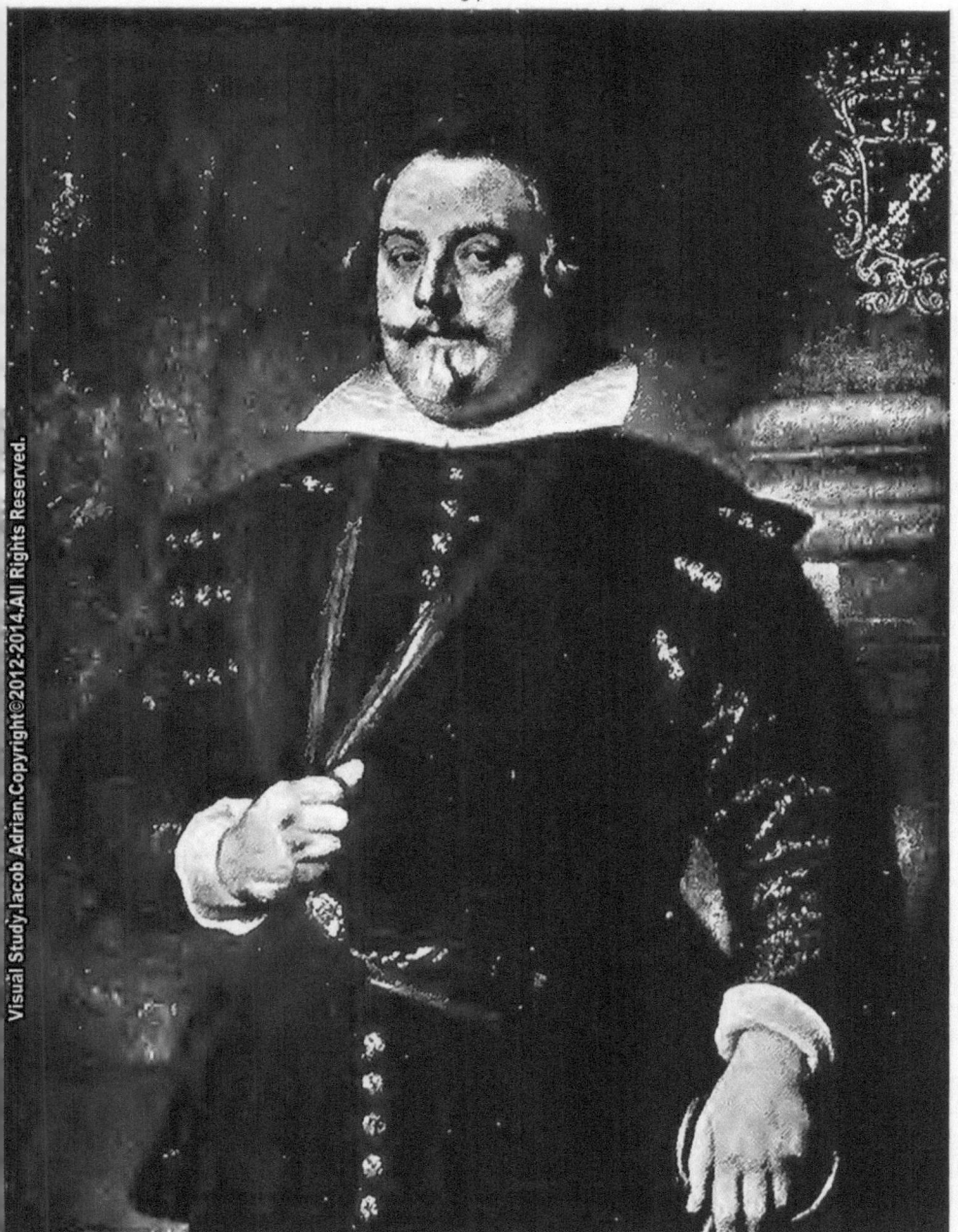

FRANCESCO DE MONCADA   FRANÇOIS DE MONCADE
(Imperial Gallery, Vienna)   *(Galerie impériale, Vienne)*
FRANCESCO DE MONCADA
(Wien, Kaiserl. Galerie)
F. Hanfstaengl, Photo.

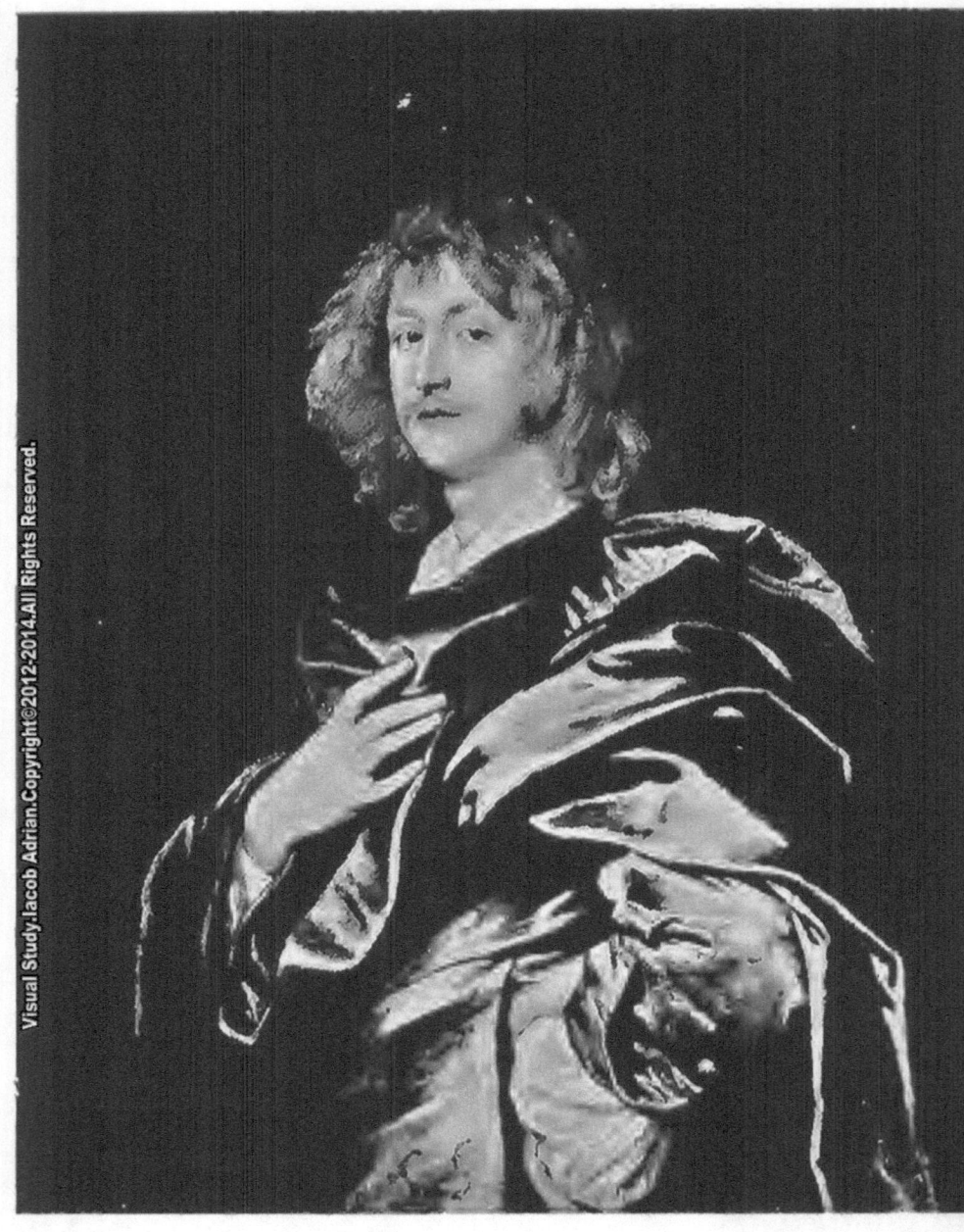

PHILIP HERBERT,
FIFTH EARL OF PEMBROKE
(*Dulwich Gallery*)

PHILIPPE HERBERT,
COMTE DE PEMBROKE
(*Galerie, Dulwich*)

PHILIP HERBERT, DER FÜNFTE GRAF VON PEMBROKE
(*Dulwich, Galerie*)
F. Hanfstaengl, Photo.

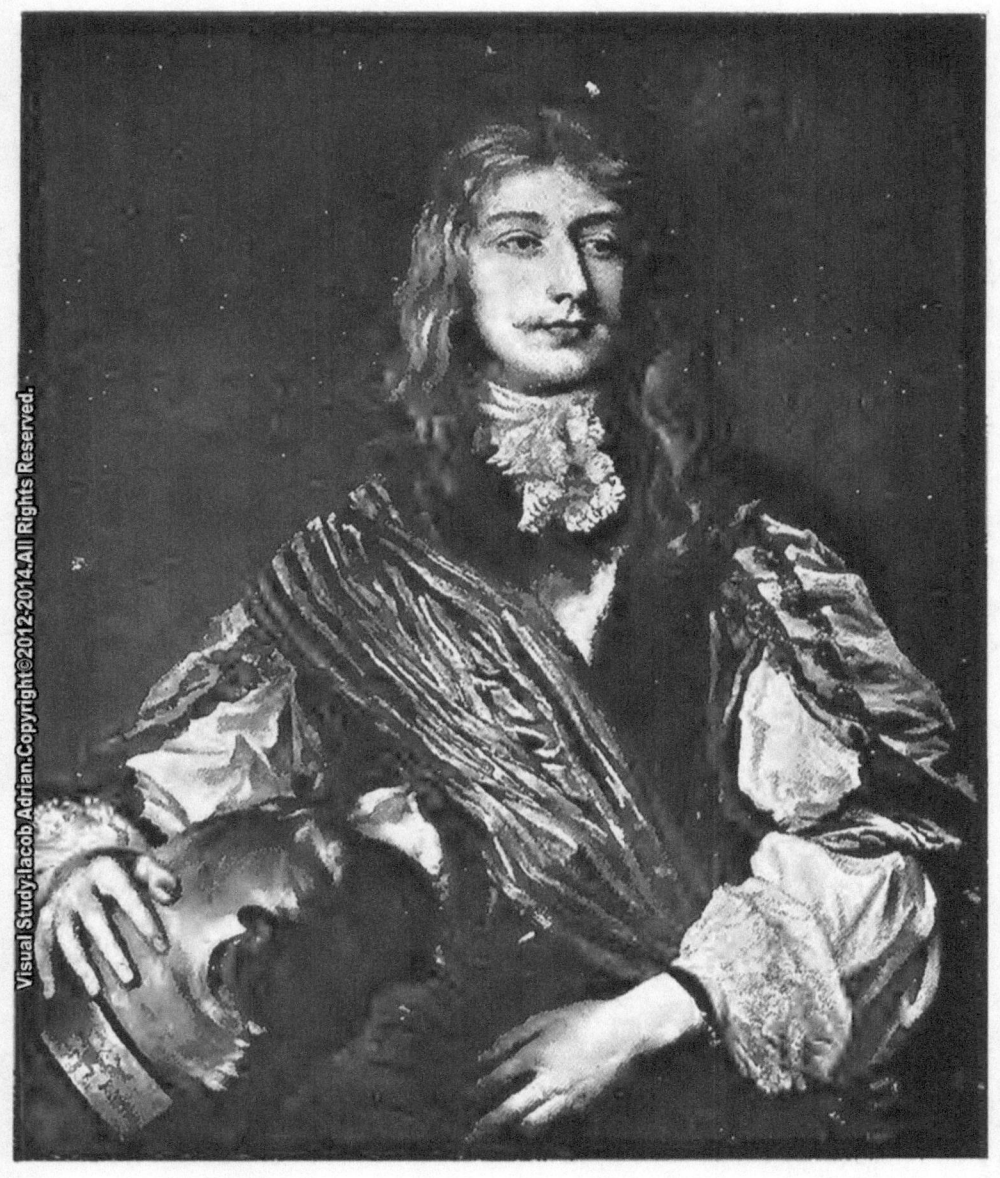

THOMAS KILLIGREW
(*Duke of Devonshire, London*)

THOMAS KILLIGREW
(*Duc de Devonshire, Londres*)

THOMAS KILLIGREW
(*London, Herzog von Devonshire*)
F. Hanfstaengl, Photo.

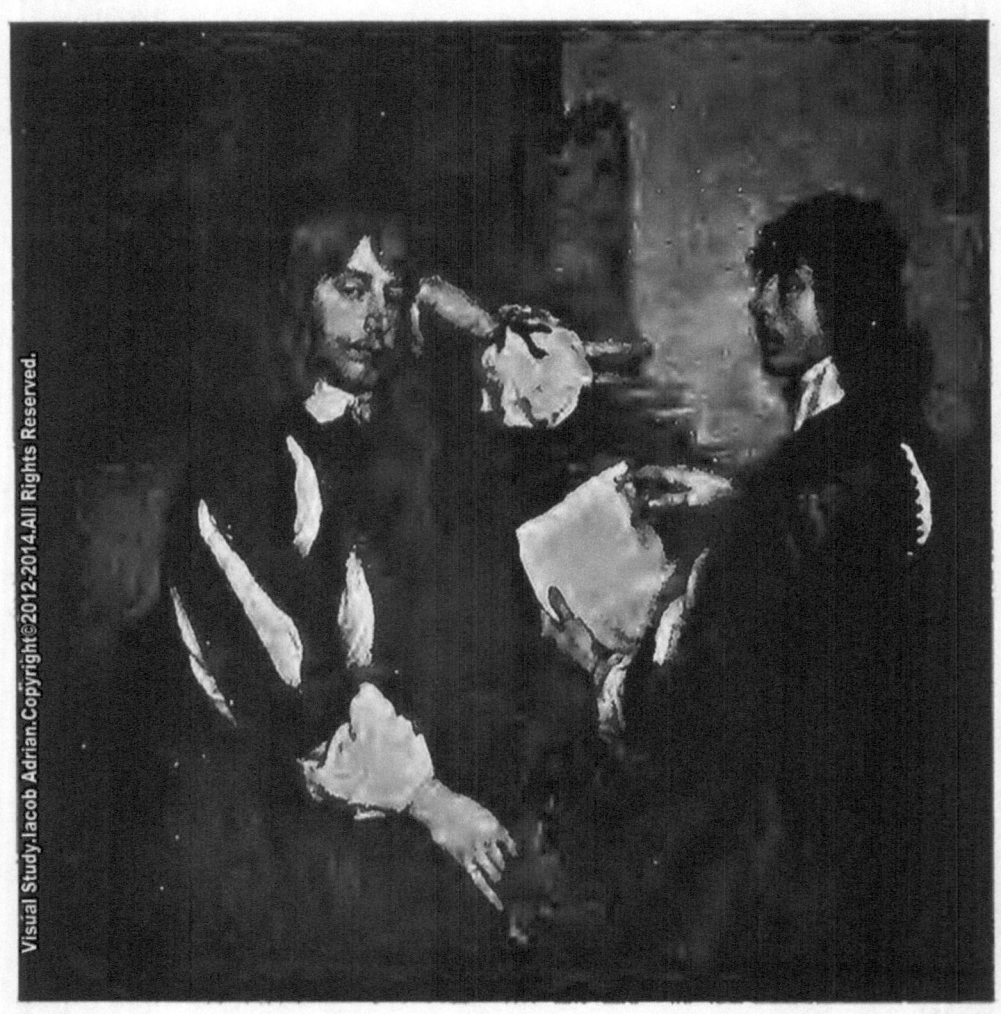

THOMAS KILLIGREW AND
THOMAS CAREW
(*Windsor Castle*)

THOMAS KILLIGREW ET
THOMAS CAREW
(*Galerie royale, Windsor*)

THOMAS KILLIGREW UND THOMAS CAREW
(*Windsor, Kgl. Schloss*)
F. Hanfstaengl, Photo.

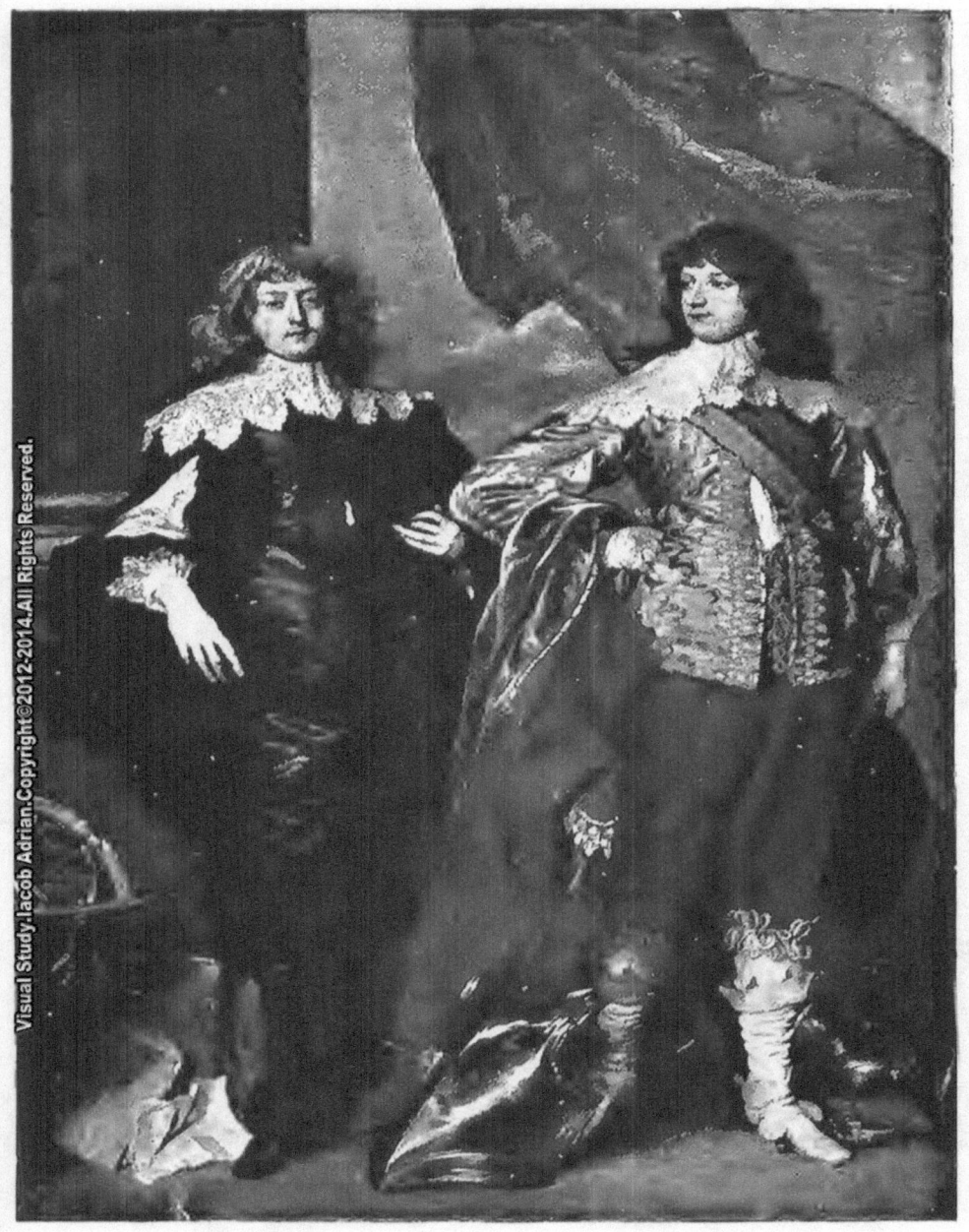

GEORGE DIGBY,
EARL OF BRISTOL, AND
WILLIAM, EARL OF BEDFORD
(*Earl Spencer, Althorp*)

GEORGE DIGBY, SECOND COMTE
DE BRISTOL ET WILLIAM,
PREMIER DUC DE BEDFORD
(*Comte Spencer, Althorp*)

GEORGE DIGBY, GRAF VON BRISTOL, UND WILLIAM,
HERZOG VON BEDFORD
(*Althorp, Graf Spencer*)   *F. Hanfstaengl, Photo.*

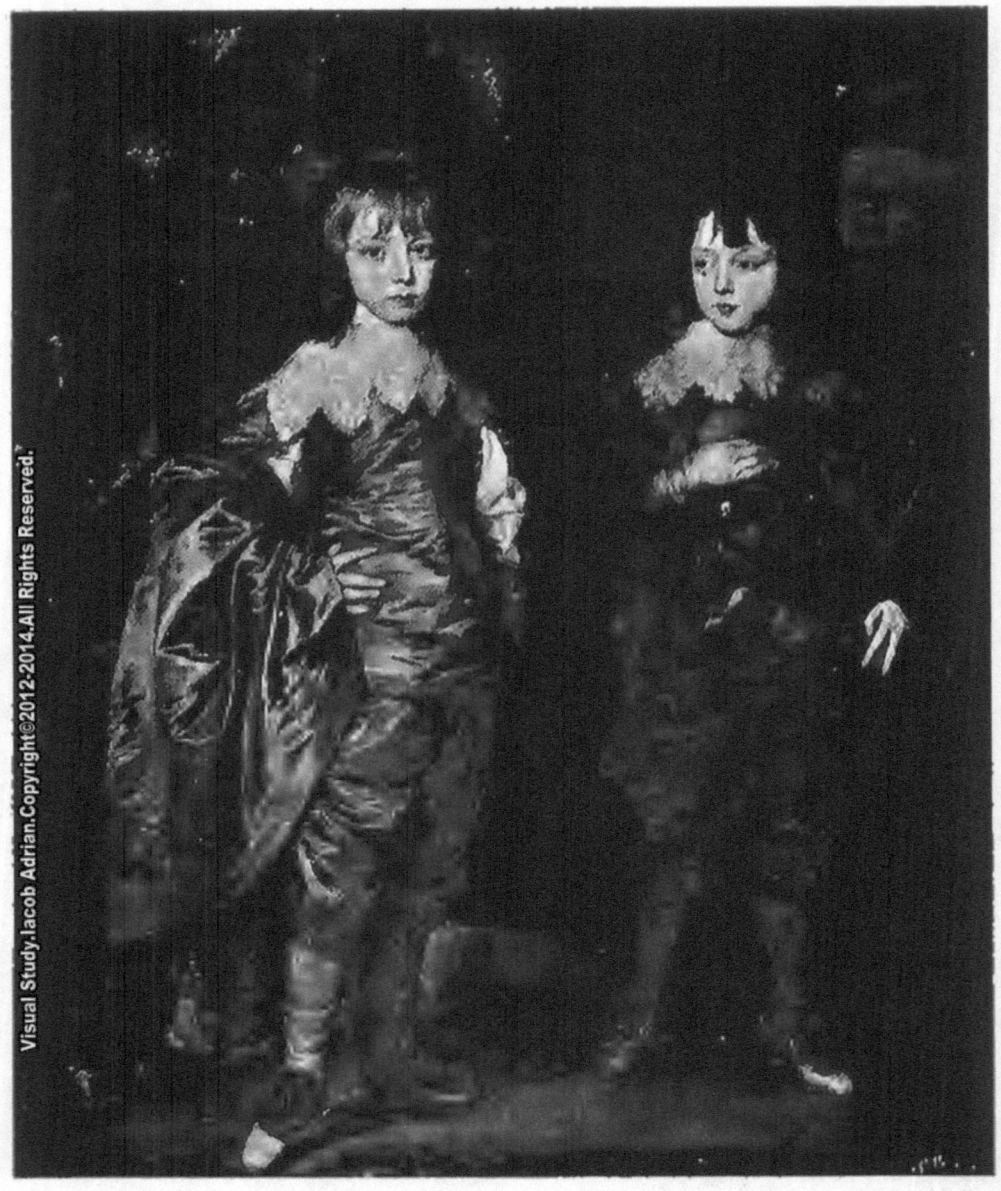

GEORGE VILLIERS, DUKE OF
BUCKINGHAM AND HIS BROTHER,
LORD FRANCIS VILLIERS
(*Windsor Castle*)

GEORGE VILLIERS, DUC DE
BUCKINGHAM ET FRANCIS VILLIERS,
FILS DU DUC DE BUCKINGHAM
(*Galerie royale, Windsor*)

GEORG VILLIERS, HERZOG VON BUCKINGHAM, UND SEIN BRUDER,
LORD FRANCIS VILLIERS
(*Windsor, Kgl. Schloss*)
F. Hanfstaengl, Photo.

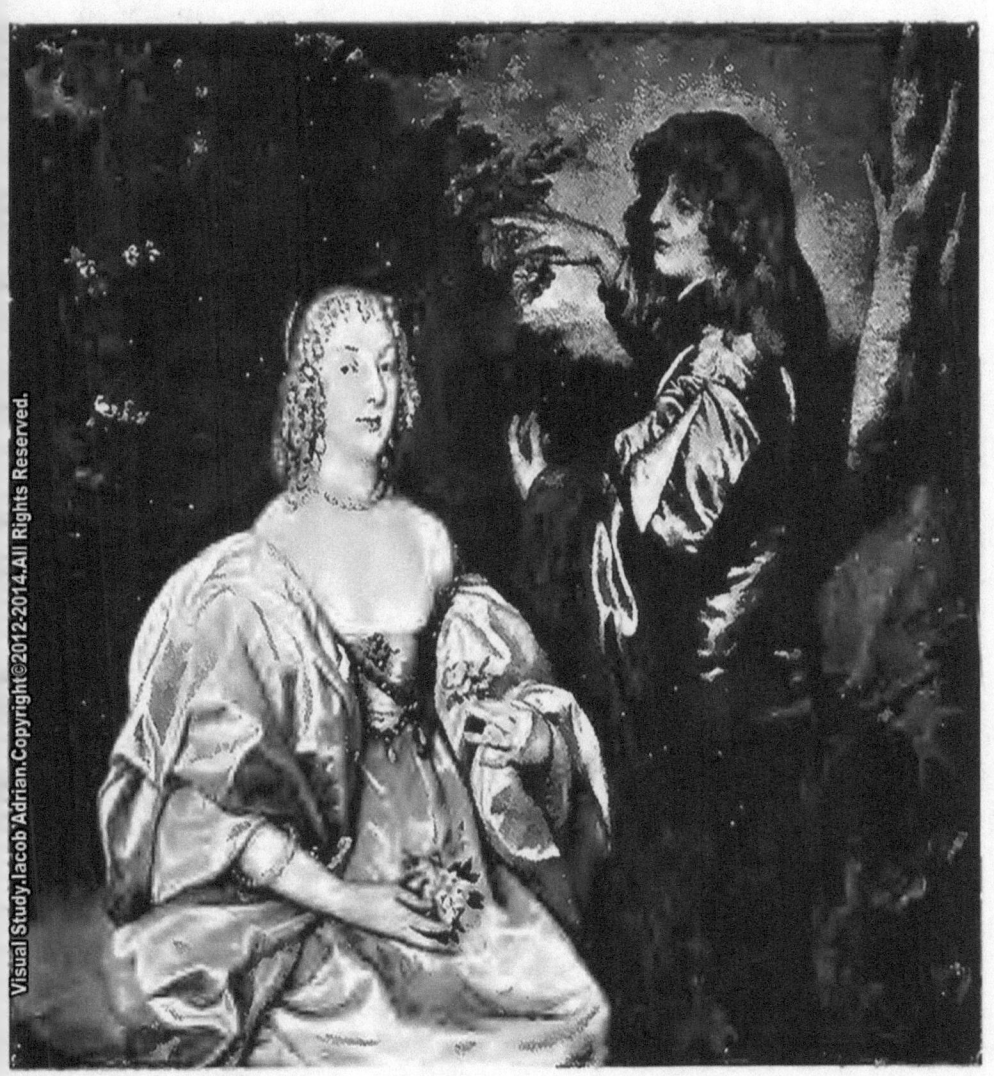

THE EARL OF PEMBROKE
AND HIS SISTER,
THE COUNTESS OF CARNARVON
(*Duke of Devonshire, London*)

LE COMTE DE PEMBROKE
ET SA SŒUR LA
COMTESSE DE CARNARVON
(*Duc de Devonshire, Londres*)

GRAF VON PEMBROKE UND SEINE SCHWESTER, GRÄFIN VON CARNARVON
(*London, Herzog von Devonshire*) *F. Hanfstaengl, Photo.*

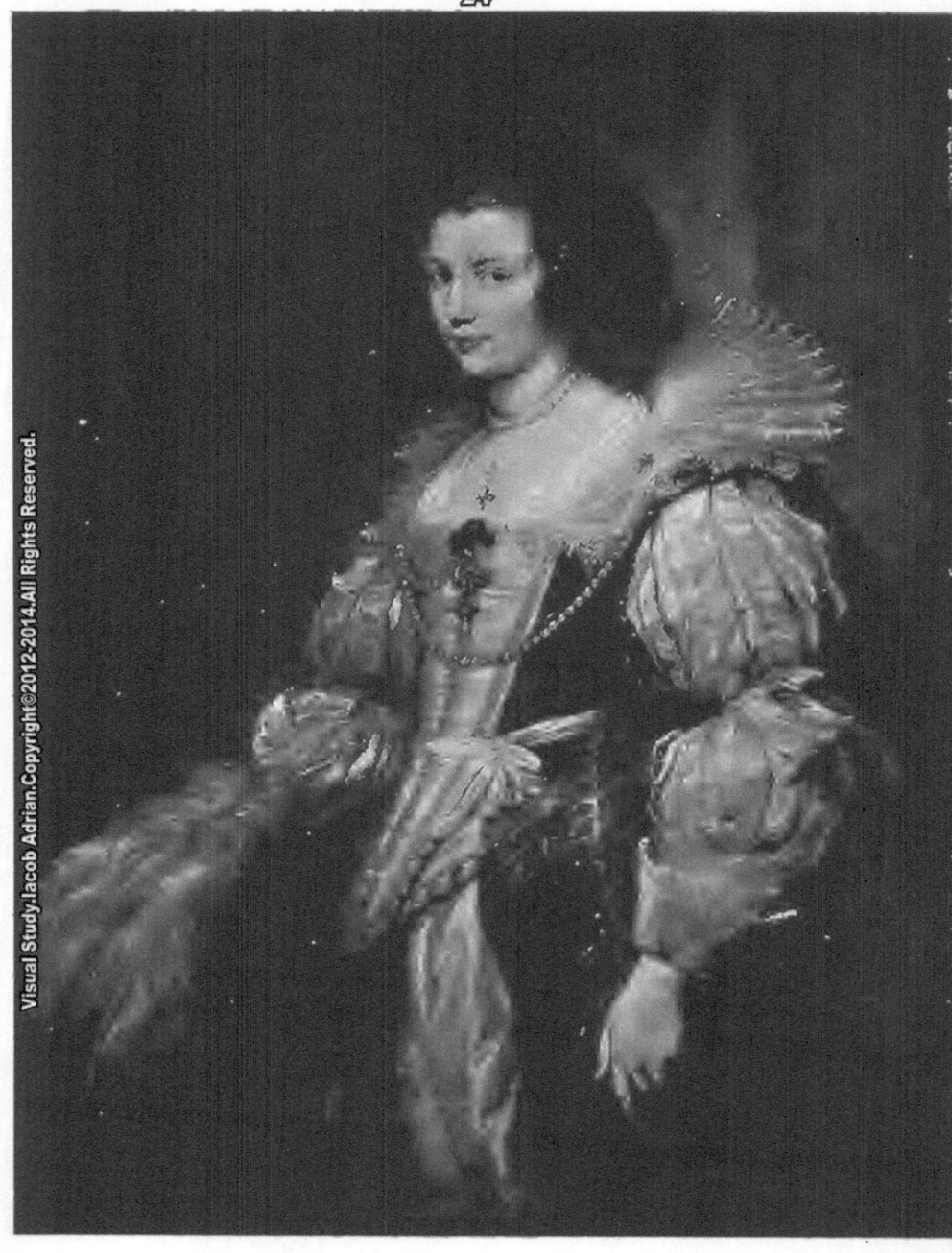

MARIA LUISE VON TASSIS   MARIE LOUISE DE TASSIS
(*Liechtenstein Gallery, Vienna*)   (*Galerie Liechtenstein, Vienne*)
MARIA LUISE VON TASSIS
(*Wien, Liechtenstein Galerie*)
F. Hanfstaengl, Photo.

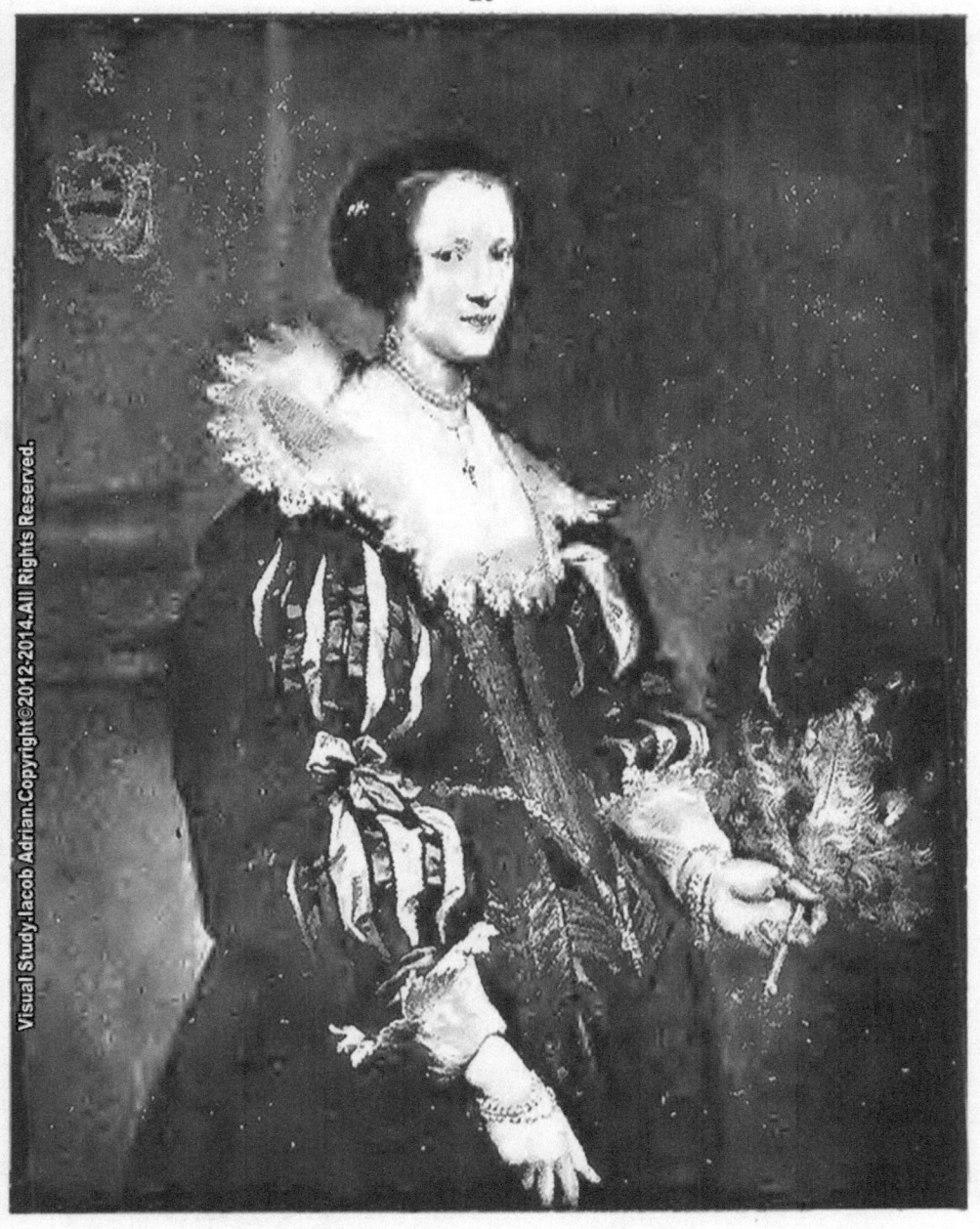

ANNA WAKE, LADY SHEFFIELD   ANNA WAKE
(Royal Gallery, The Hague)   *(Musée royal, La Haye)*
ANNA WAKE, LADY SHEFFIELD
(Haag, Kgl. Galerie)
F. Hanfstaengl, Photo.

26

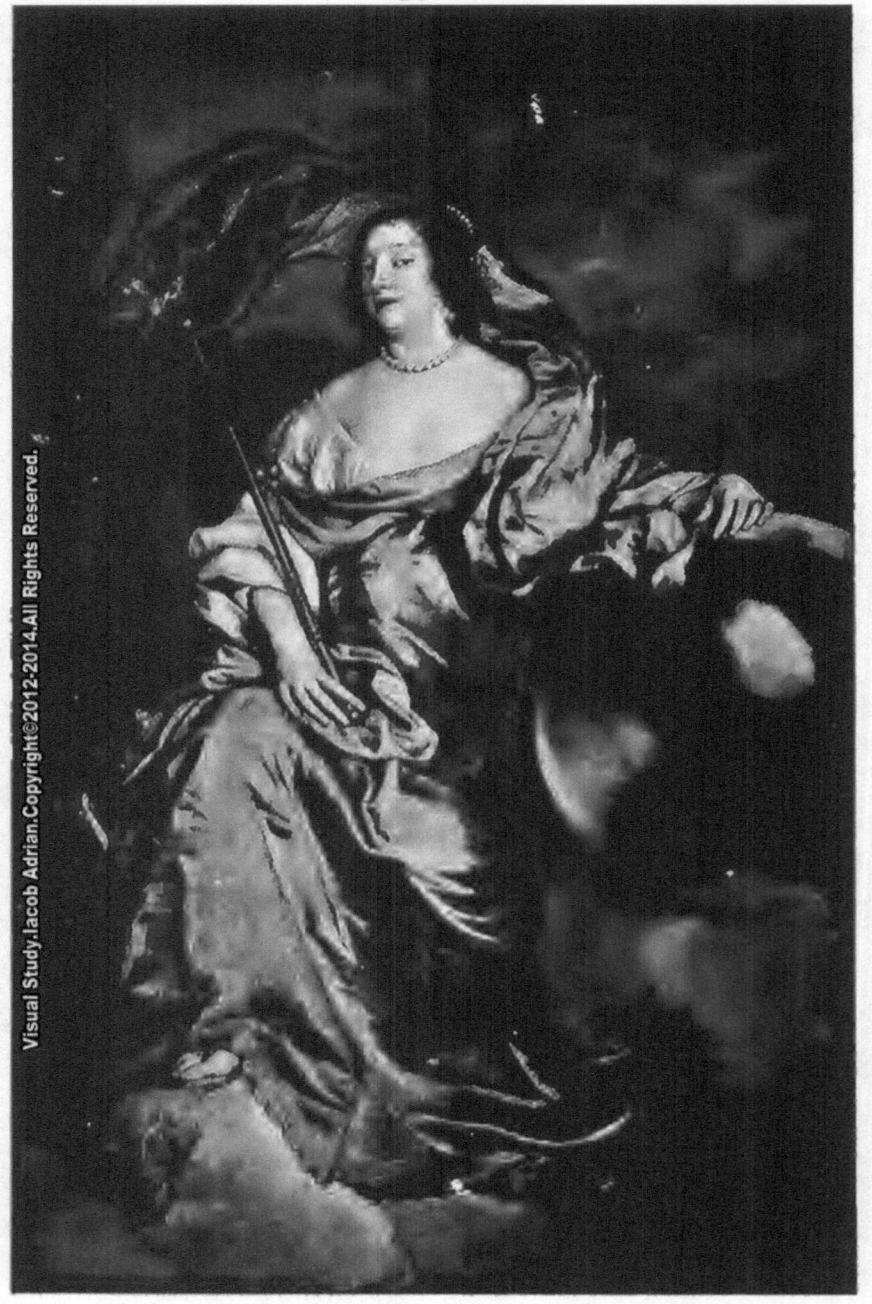

THE COUNTESS OF SOUTHAMPTON   LA COMTESSE DE SOUTHAMPTON
(*Earl Spencer, Althorp*)   (*Comte Spencer, Althorp*)
GRÄFIN VON SOUTHAMPTON
(*Althorp, Graf Spencer*)
F. Hanfstuengl, Photo.

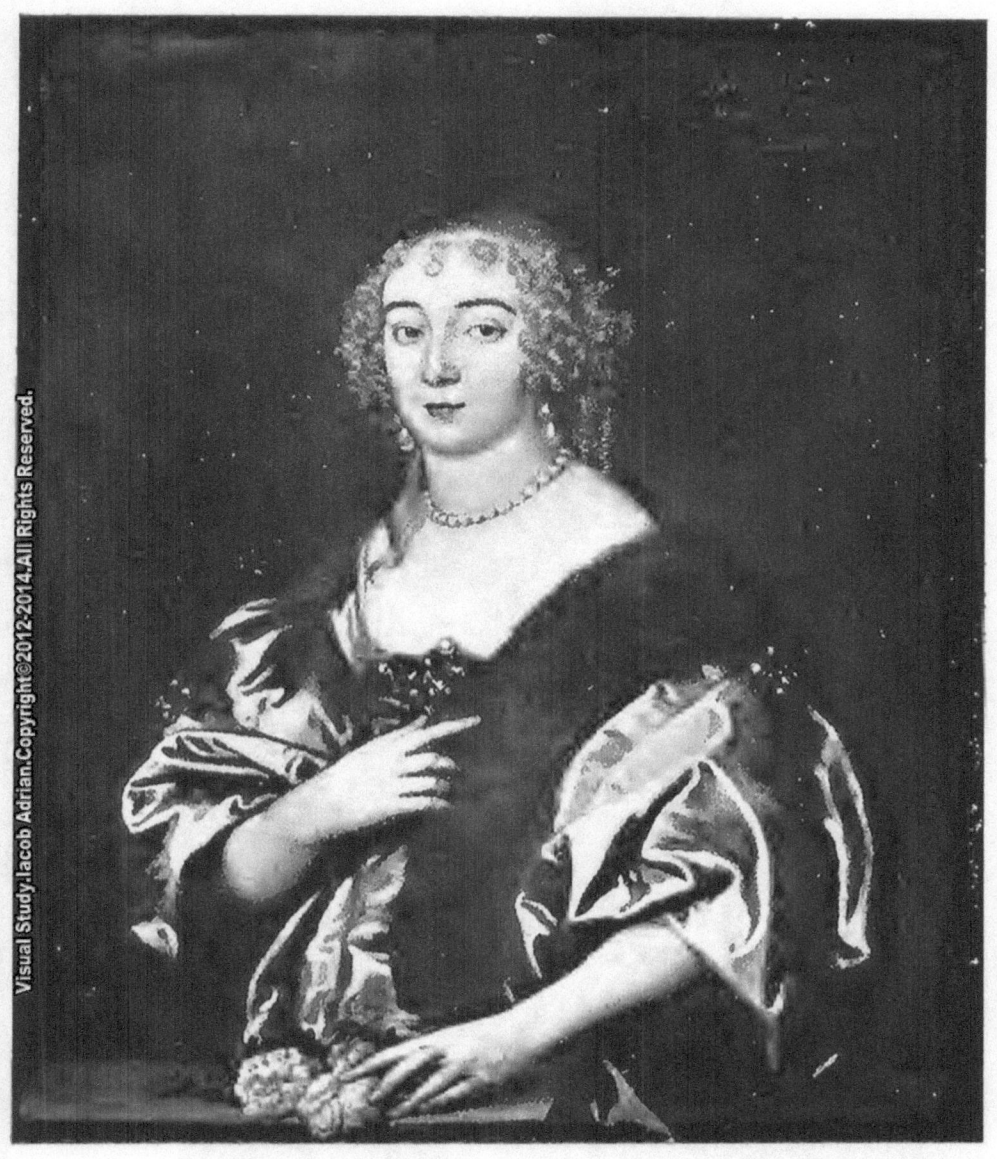

DOROTHEA, FIRST COUNTESS   DOROTHÉE SIDNEY,
OF SUNDERLAND   COMTESSE DE SUNDERLAND
(*Earl Spencer, Althorp*)   (*Comte Spencer, Althorp*)
DOROTHEA, ERSTE GRÄFIN VON SUNDERLAND
(*Althorp, Graf Spencer*)
F. Hanfstaengl, Photo.

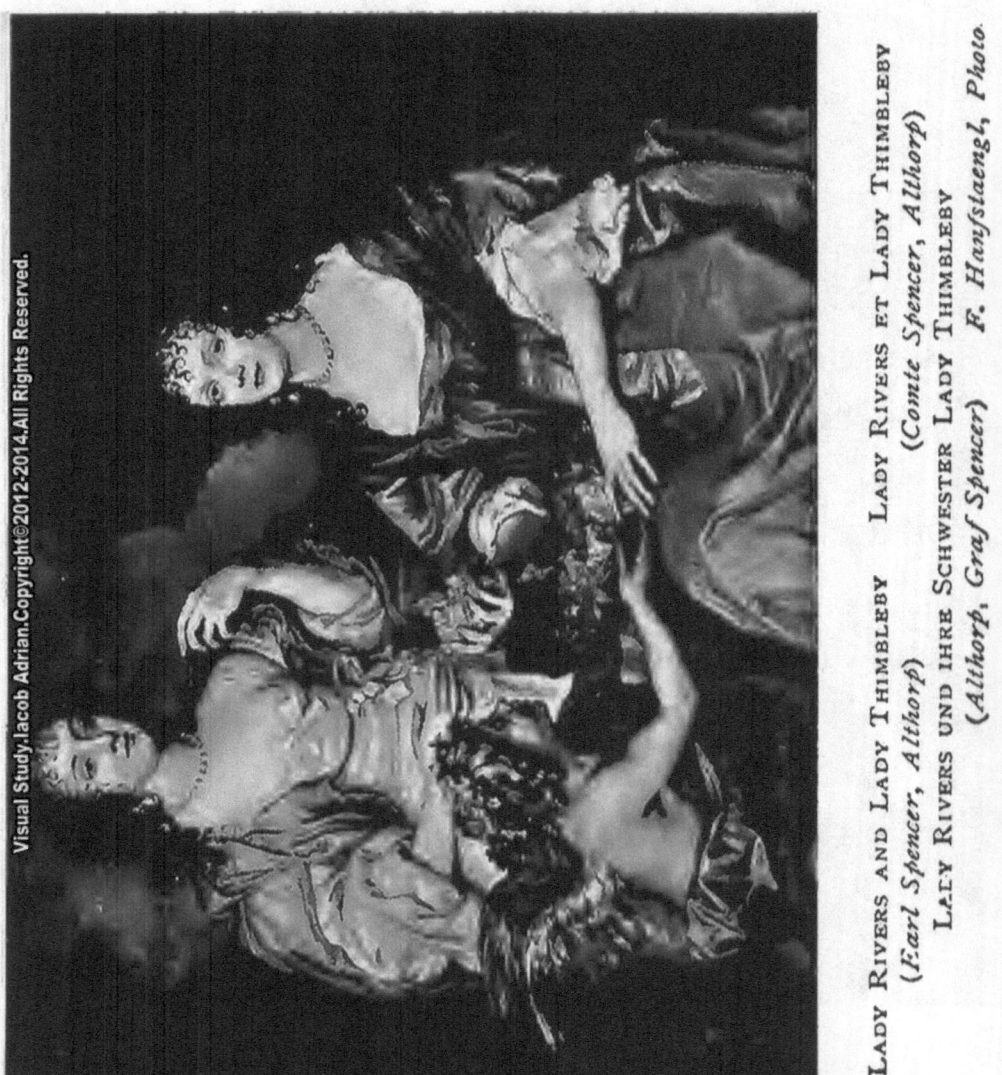

LADY RIVERS AND LADY THIMBLEBY   LADY RIVERS ET LADY THIMBLEBY
(Earl Spencer, Althorp)   (Comte Spencer, Althorp)
LADY RIVERS UND IHRE SCHWESTER LADY THIMBLEBY
(Althorp, Graf Spencer)   F. Hanfstaengl, Photo.

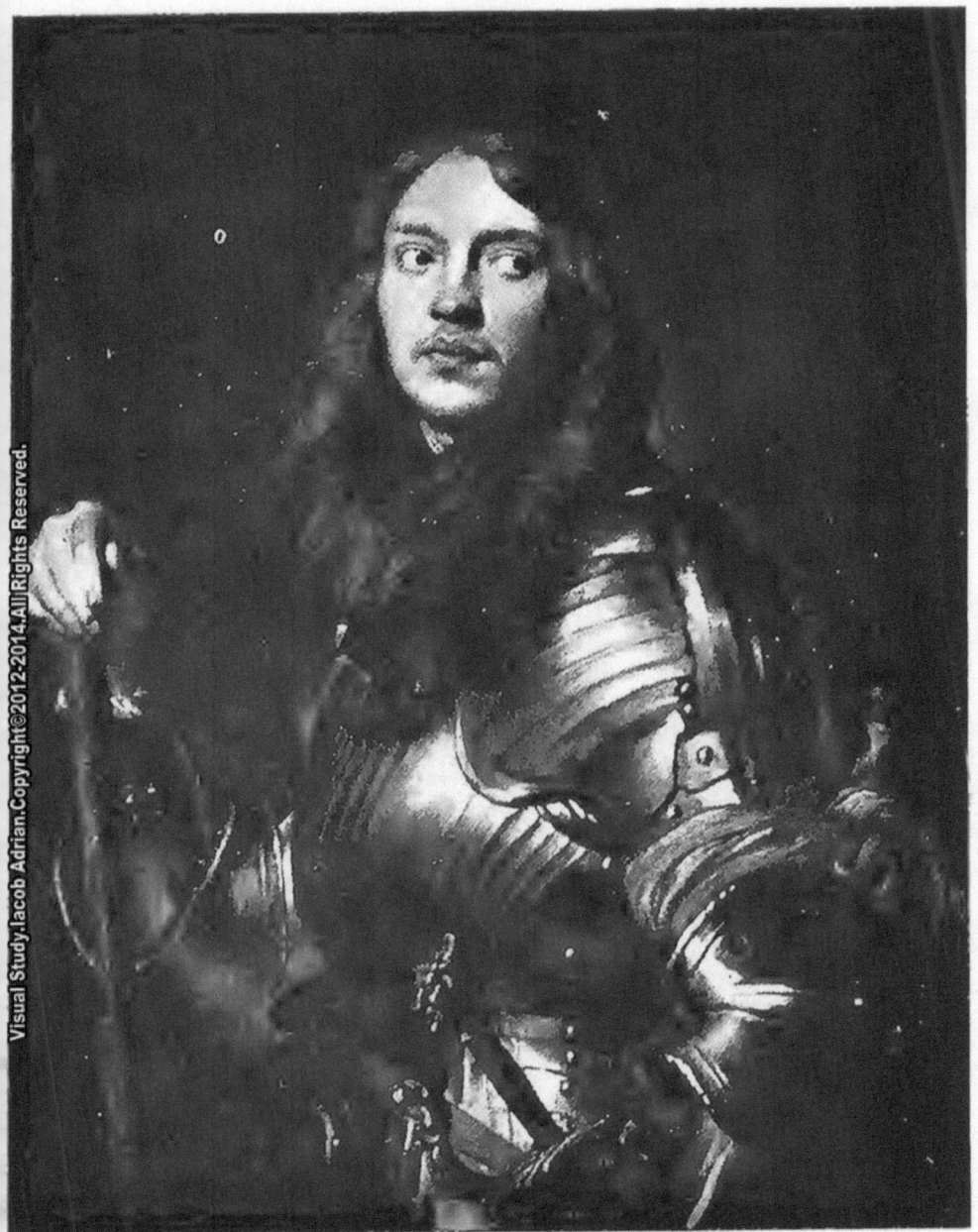

PORTRAIT OF A GENERAL
WITH A RED SCARF
(*Royal Gallery, Dresden*)

HOMME EN CUIRASSE,
TENANT UN BÂTON
(*Galerie royale, Dresde*)

BILDNIS EINES FELDHERRN MIT ROTER ARMBINDE
(*Dresden, Kgl. Galerie*)
F. Hanfstaengl, Photo

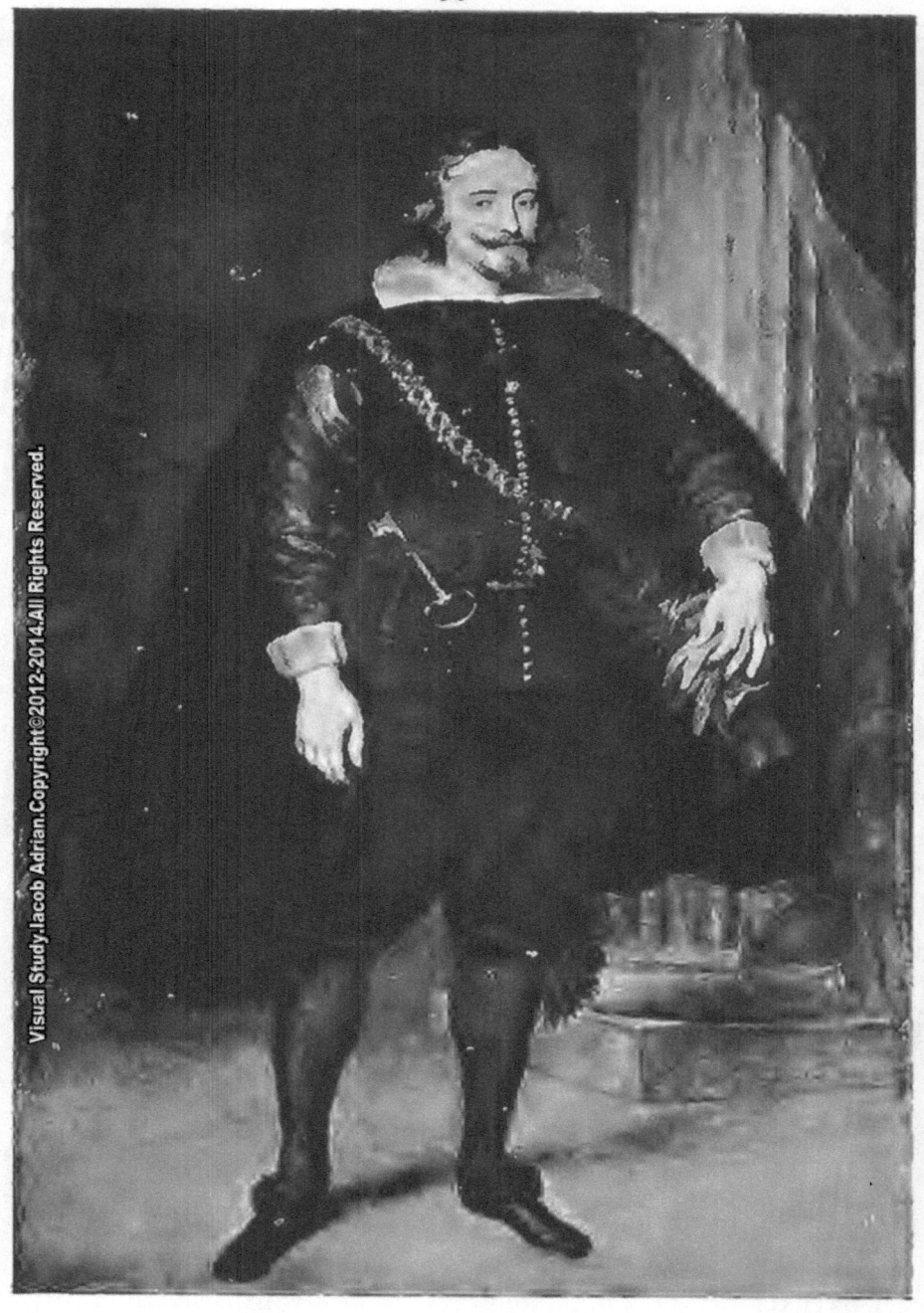

PETER PAUL RUBENS
(Earl Spencer, Althorp)

PIERRE-PAUL RUBENS
(Comte Spencer, Althorp)

PETER PAUL RUBENS
(Althorp, Graf Spencer)
F. Hanfstaengl, Photo

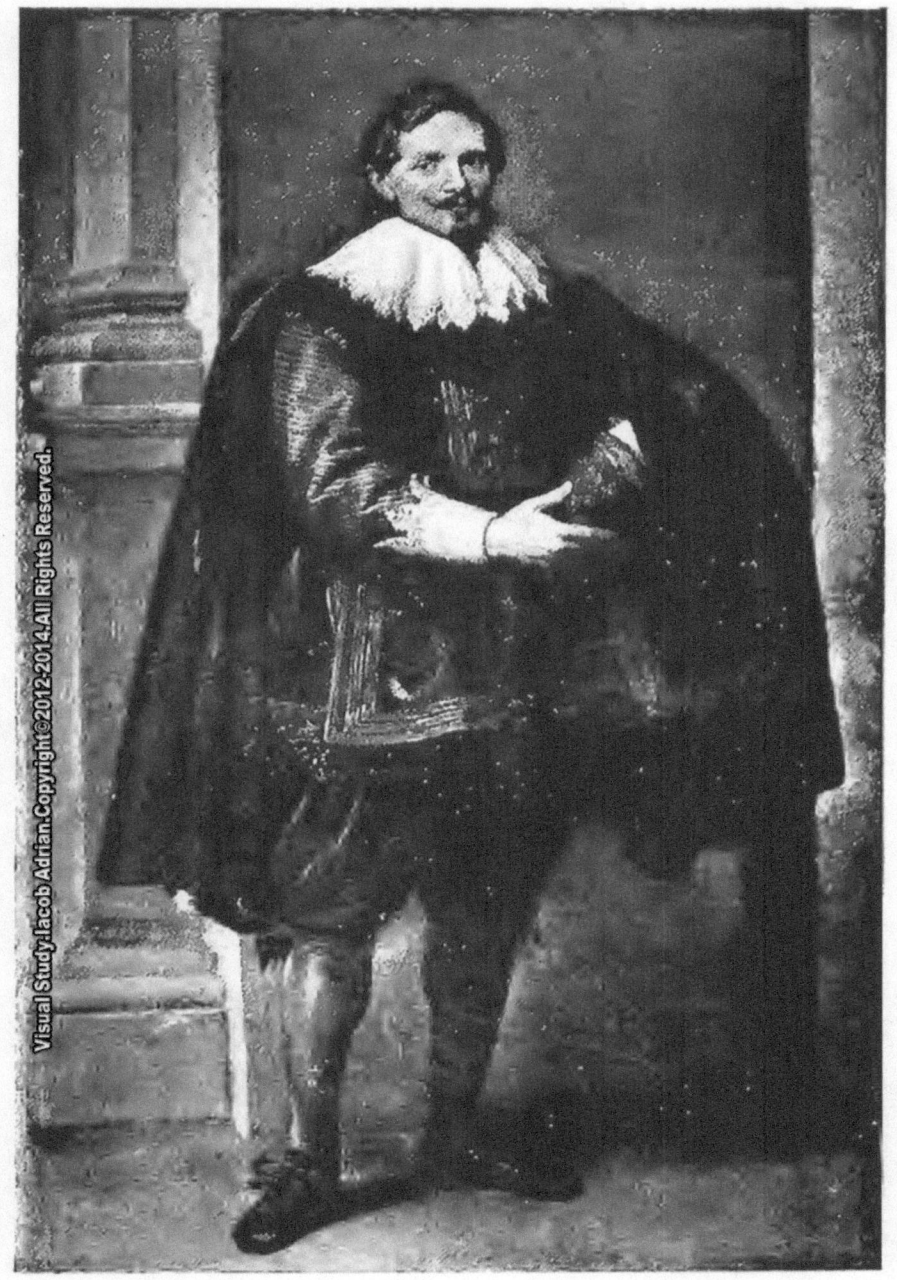

THE BURGOMASTER
OF ANTWERP
(*Pinakothek, Munich*)

LE BOURGMESTRE
D'ANVERS
(*Pinacothèque, Munich*)

DER BÜRGERMEISTER VON ANTWERPEN
(*München, Pinakothek*)
F. Hanfstaengl, Photo.

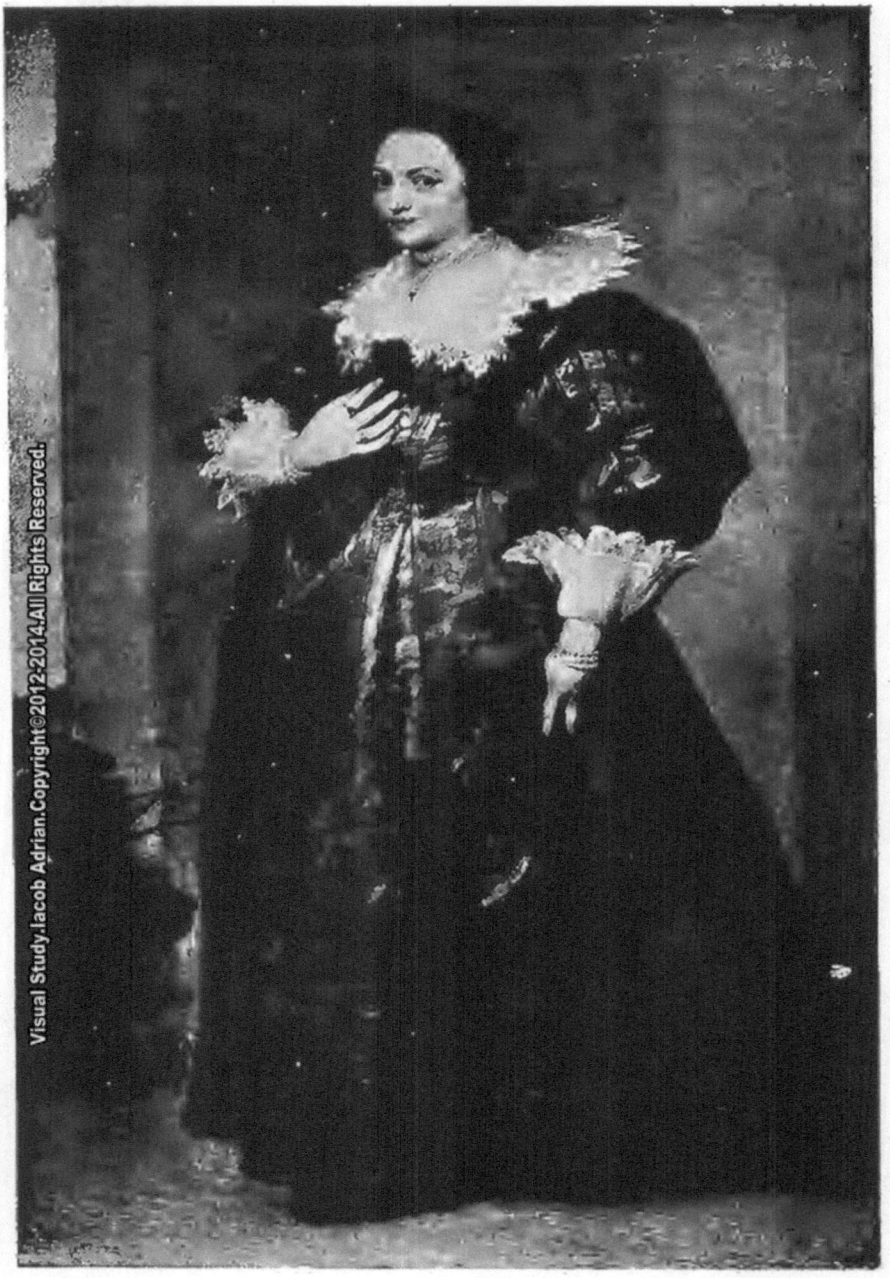

THE BURGOMASTER OF
ANTWERP'S WIFE
(*Pinakothek, Munich*)

LA FEMME DU BOURGMESTRE
D'ANVERS
(*Pinacothèque, Munich*)

DIE FRAU DES BÜRGERMEISTERS VON ANTWERPEN
(*München, Pinakothek*)
F. Hanfstaengl, Photo.

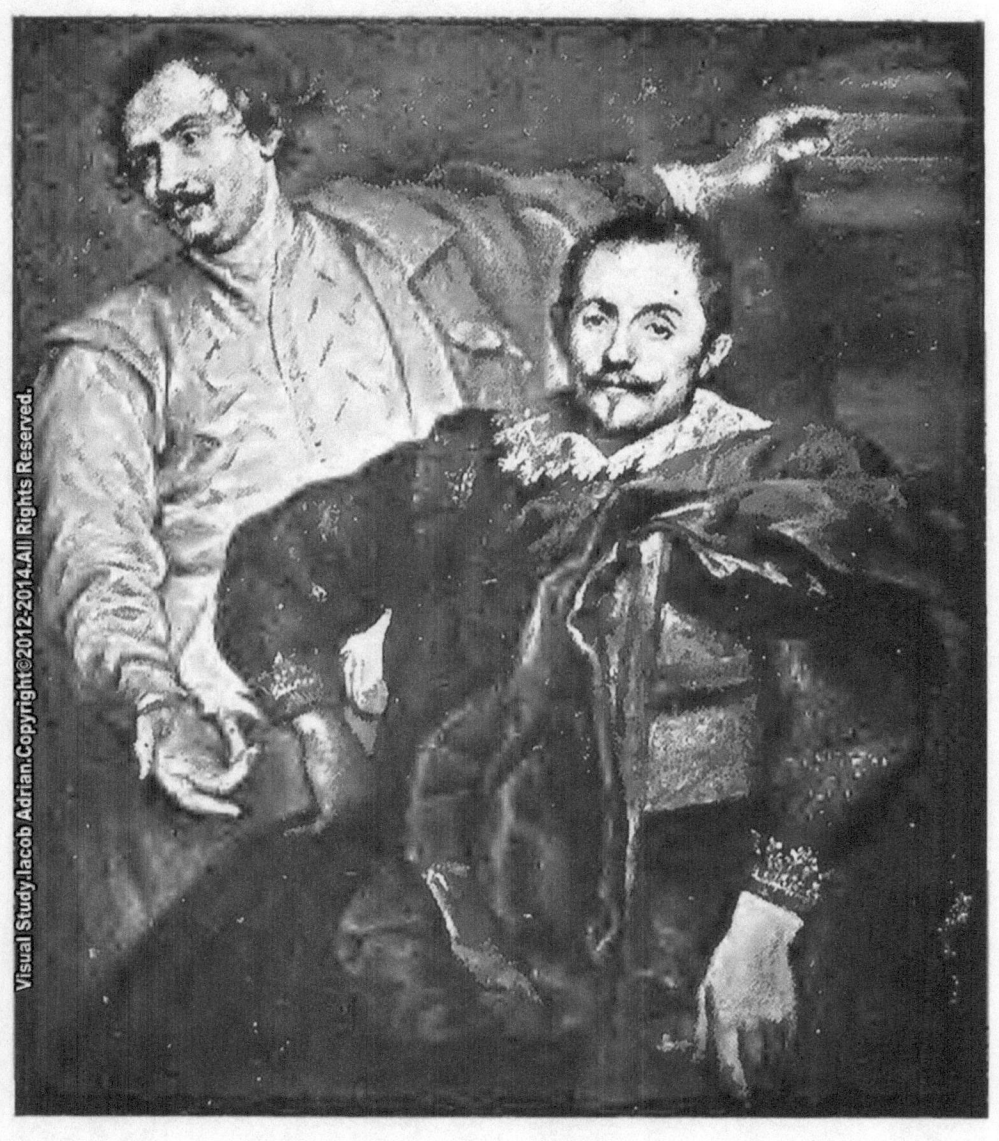

THE BROTHERS LUCAS AND   LES FRÈRES LUCAS ET CORNÉLIUS
CORNELIUS DE WAEL   DE WAEL
(*Royal Gallery, Cassel*)   (*Galerie royale, Cassel*)
DIE BRÜDER LUKAS UND CORNELIS DE WAEL
(*Cassel, Kgl. Galerie*)
F. Hanfstaengl, Photo.

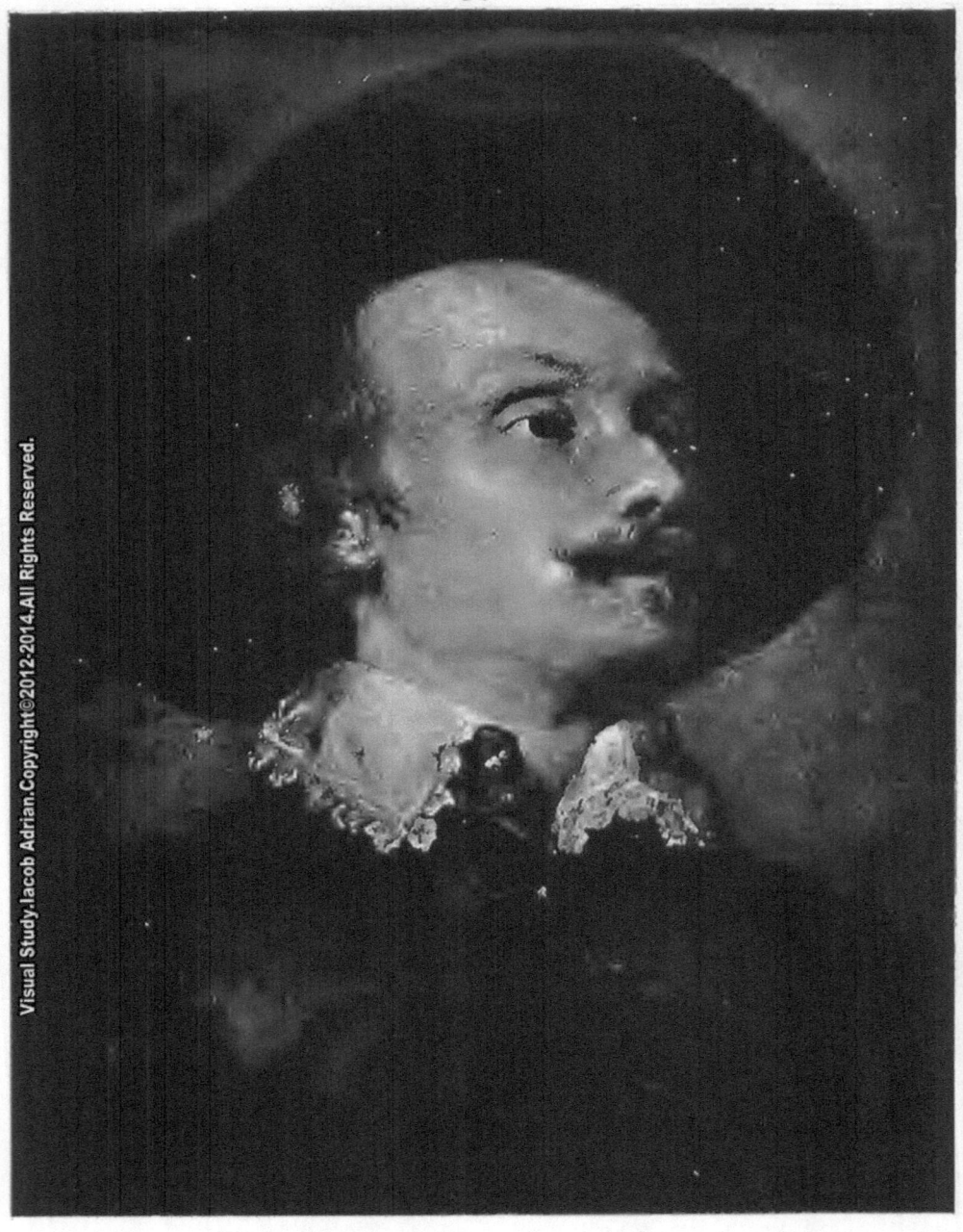

P. SNAYERS, BATTLE AND   P. SNAYERS, PEINTRE DE BATAILLE
LANDSCAPE PAINTER   ET DE PAYSAGE
(*Pinakoth:k, Munich*)   (*Pinacothèque, Munich*)
P. SNAYERS, SCHLACHTEN- UND LANDSCHAFTSMALER
(*München, Pinakothek*)
F. Hanfstaengl, Photo.

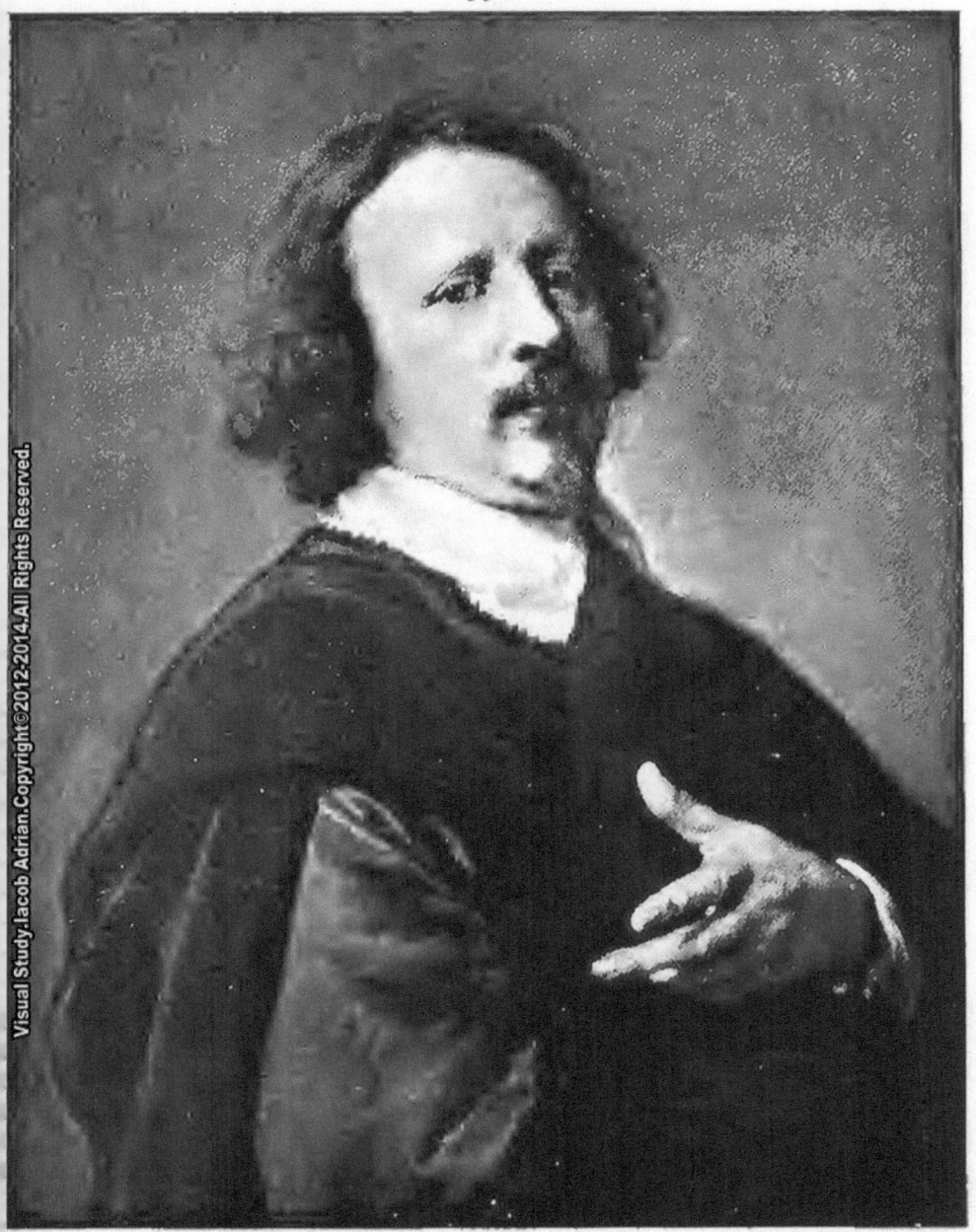

PICTURE OF CASPAR CRAYER,
THE ARTIST
(*Liechtenstein Gallery, Vienna*)

PORTRAIT DU PEINTER
GASPARD CRAYER
(*Galerie Liechtenstein, Vienne*)

BILDNIS DES MALERS KASPAR CRAYER
(*Wien, Galerie Liechtenstein*)
F. Hanfstaengl, Photo.

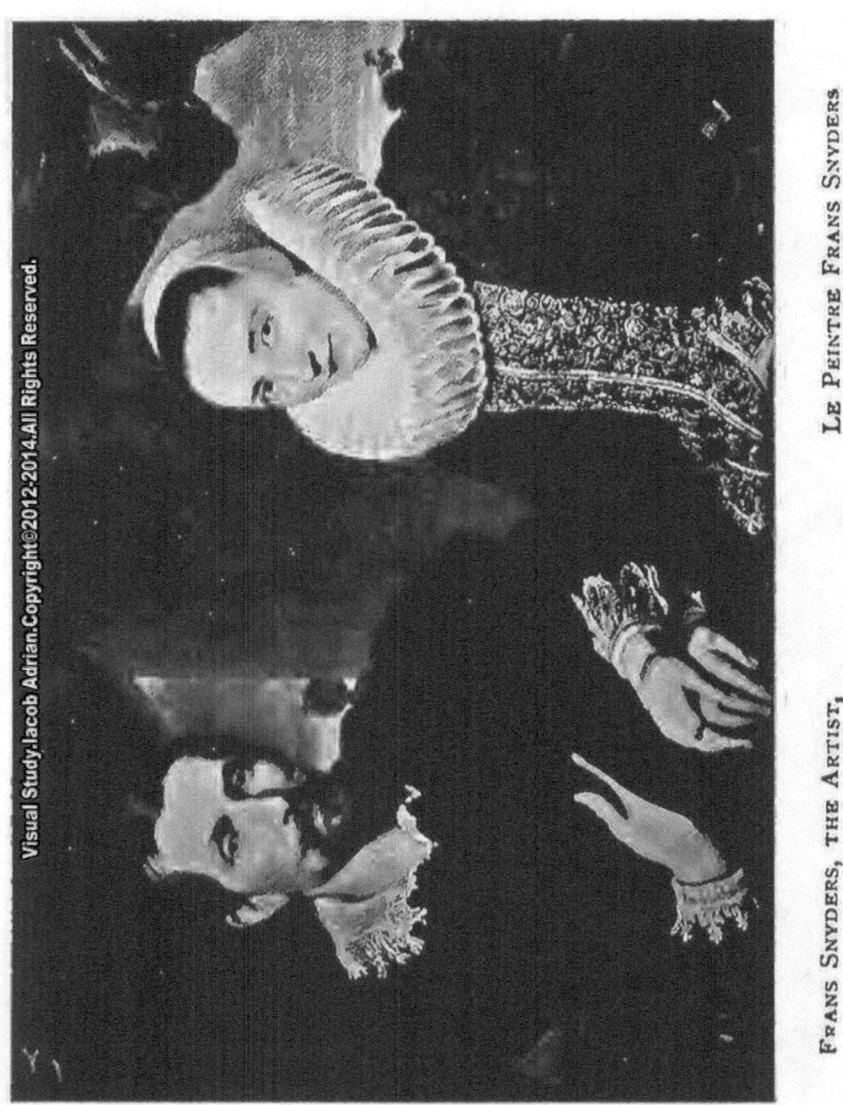

FRANS SNYDERS, THE ARTIST,
AND HIS WIFE
(*Royal Gallery, Cassel*)

LE PEINTRE FRANS SNYDERS
ET SA FEMME
(*Galerie royale, Cassel*)

DER MALER FRANS SNYDERS UND SEINE FRAU
(*Cassel, Kgl. Galerie*)

F. Hanfstaengl, Photo.

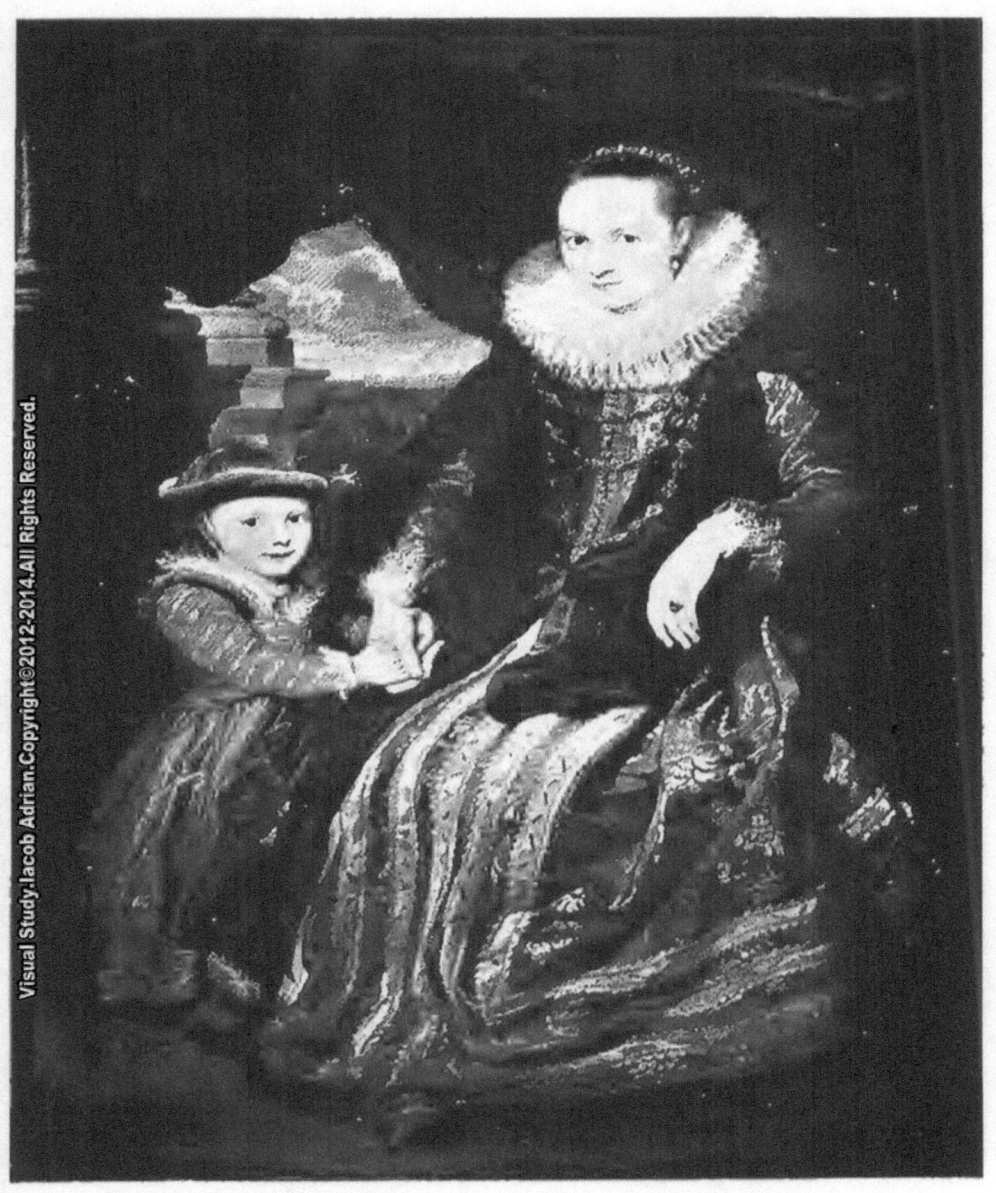

SUSANNE FOURMENT AND HER
DAUGHTER KATHARINA
(*The Hermitage, St. Petersburg*)

SUSANNE FOURMENT ET SA
FILLE KATHARINA
(*L'Ermitage, Saint-Pétersbourg*)

SUSANNE FOURMENT MIT IHRER TOCHTER KATHARINA
(*Petersburg, Eremitage*)
F. Hanfstaengl, Photo.

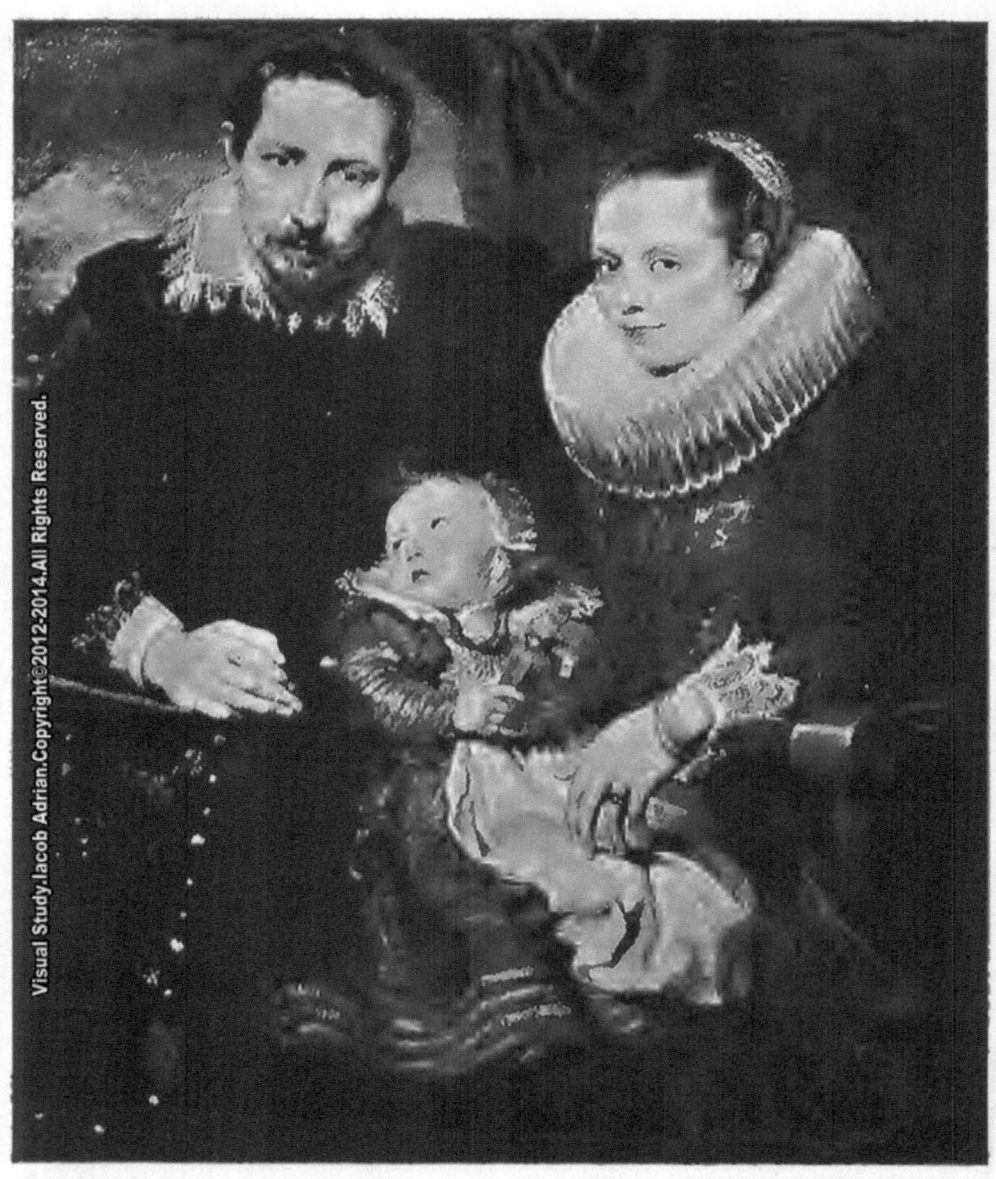

FAMILY GROUP   GROUPE DE FAMILLE
(*The Hermitage, St. Petersburg*)   (*L'Ermitage, Saint-Pétersbourg*)
FAMILIENBILDNIS
(*Petersburg, Eremitage*)
F. Hanfstaengl, Photo.

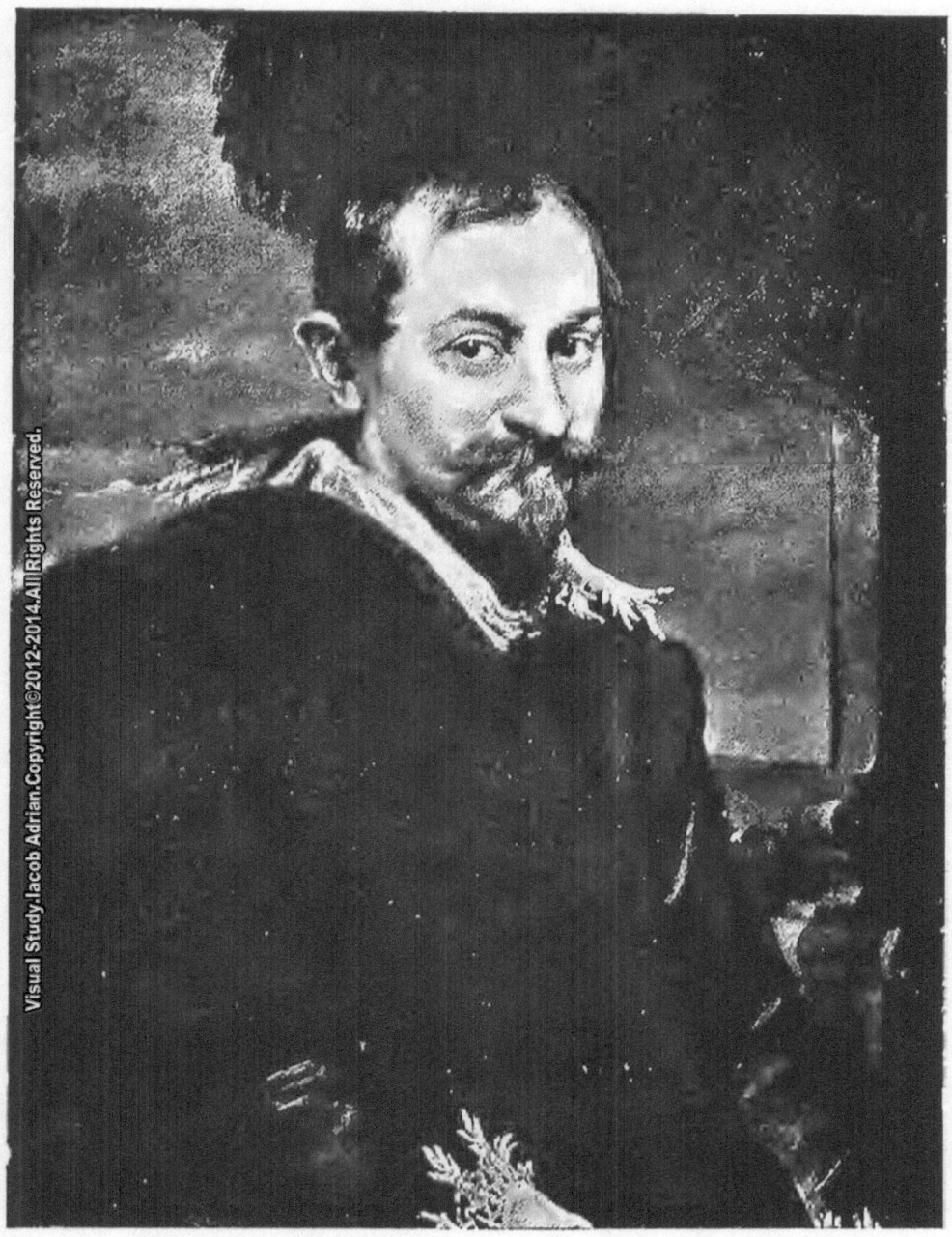

PORTRAIT OF A MAN   PORTRAIT D'HOMME
(*Imperial Gallery, Vienna*)   (*Galerie impériale, Vienne*)
BILDNIS EINES MANNES
(*Wien, Kaiserl. Galerie*)
F. Hanfstaengl, Photo.

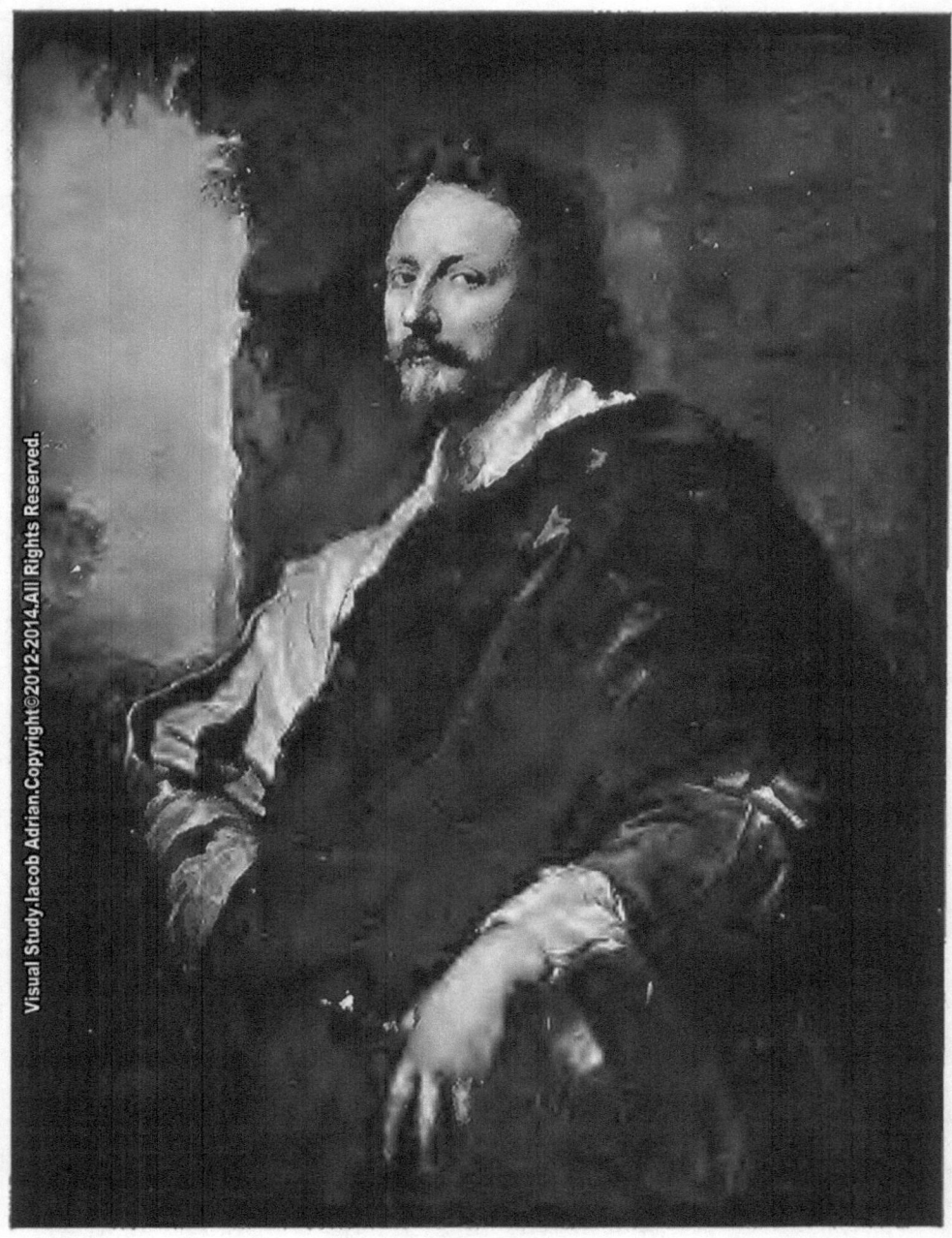

PORTRAIT OF A MAN   PORTRAIT D'HOMME
(Imperial Gallery, Vienna)   *(Galerie impériale, Vienne)*
BILDNIS EINES MANNES
(Wien, Kaiserl. Galerie)
F. Hanfstaengl, Photo.

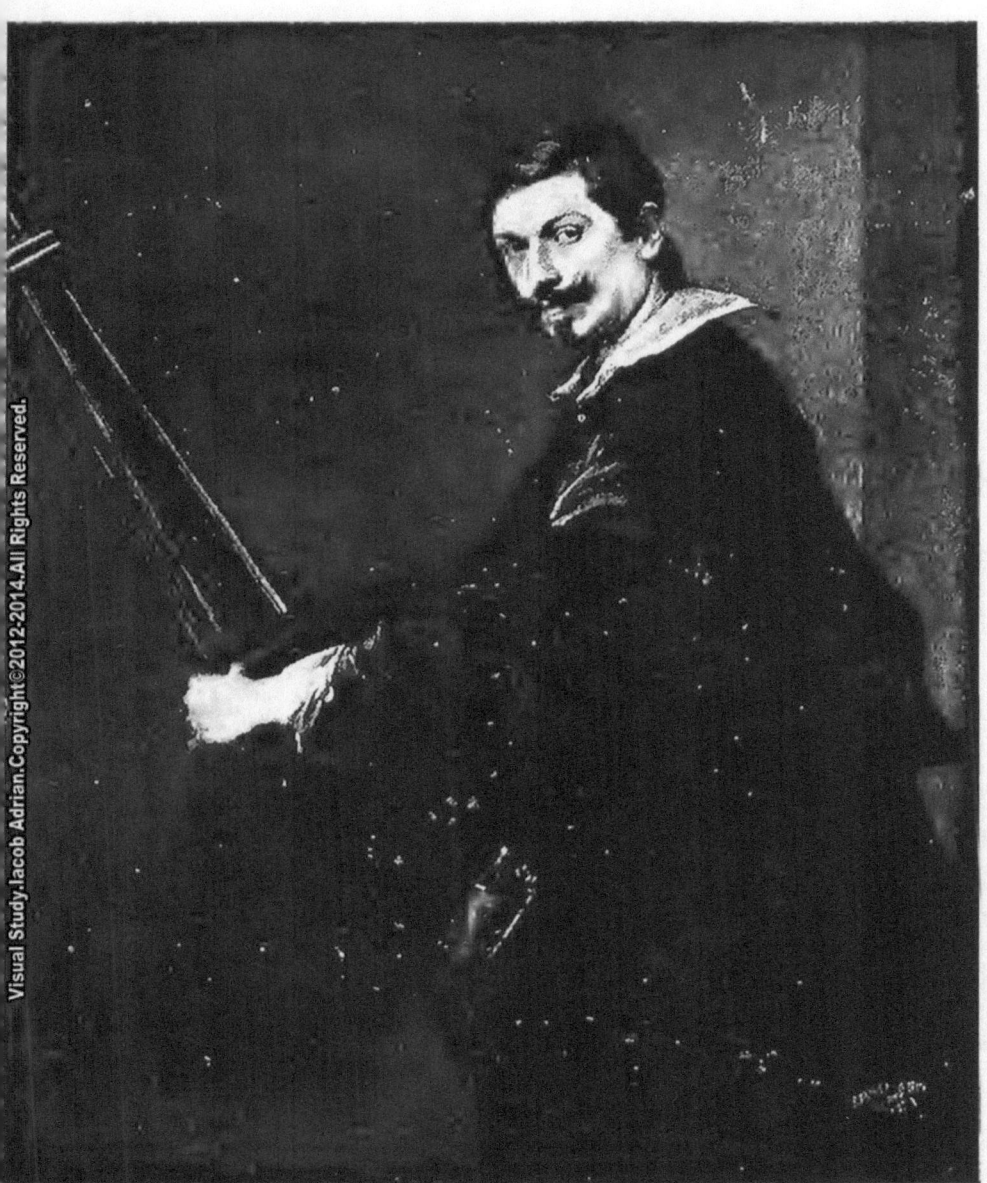

THE THEORBO-PLAYER
(*Prado, Madrid*)

LE JOUEUR DE THÉORBE
(*Prado, Madrid*)

DER THEORBESPIELER
(*Madrid, Prado*)

F. Hanfstaengl, Photo.

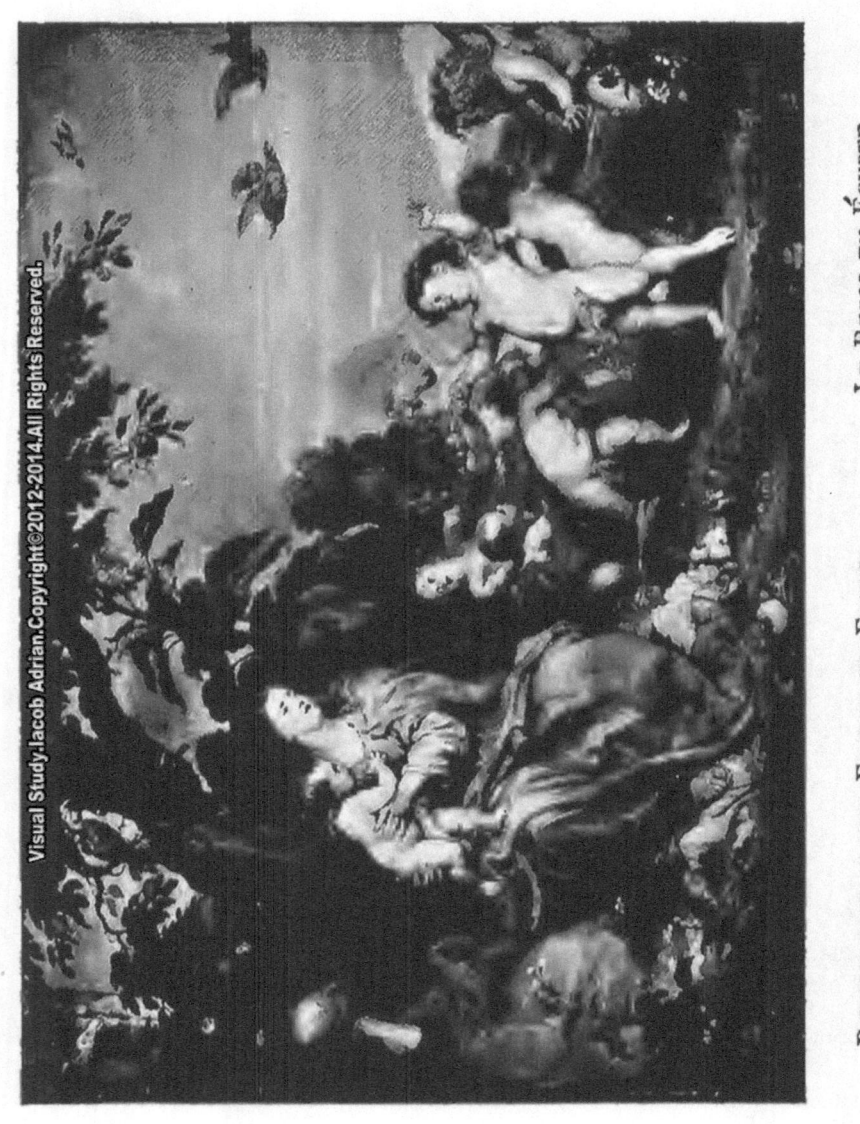

REPOSE DURING THE FLIGHT TO EGYPT   LE REPOS EN ÉGYPTE
(*The Hermitage, St. Petersburg*)   (*L'Ermitage, Saint-Pétersbourg*)
RUHE AUF DER FLUCHT NACH EGYPTEN
(*Petersburg, Eremitage*)
F. Hanfstaengl, Photo.

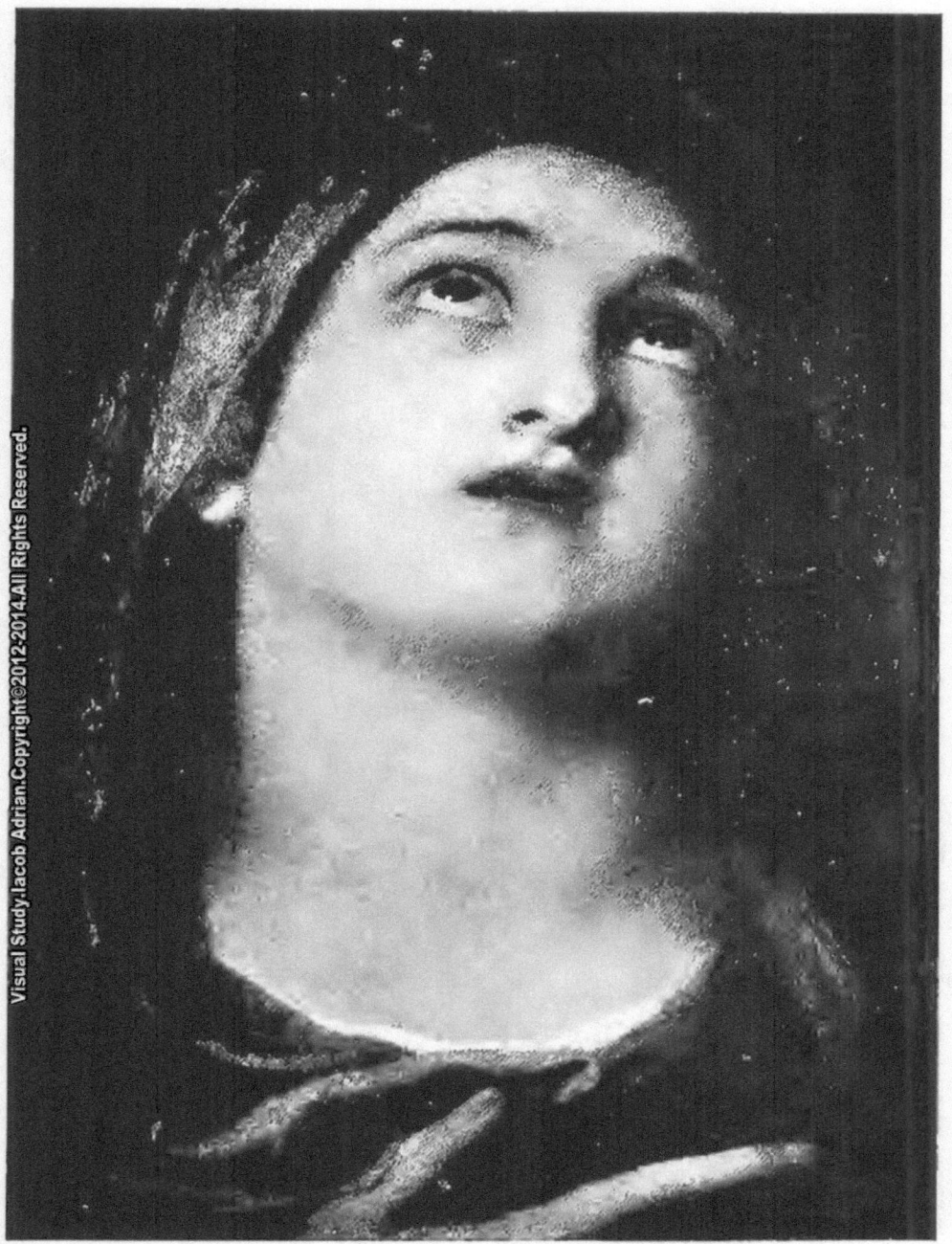

HEAD OF THE VIRGIN
(*Pitti Gallery, Florence*)

TÊTE DE LA VIERGE
(*Galerie Pitti, Florence*)

KOPF DER MADONNA
(*Florenz, Galerie Pitti*)

F. Hanfstaengl, Photo.

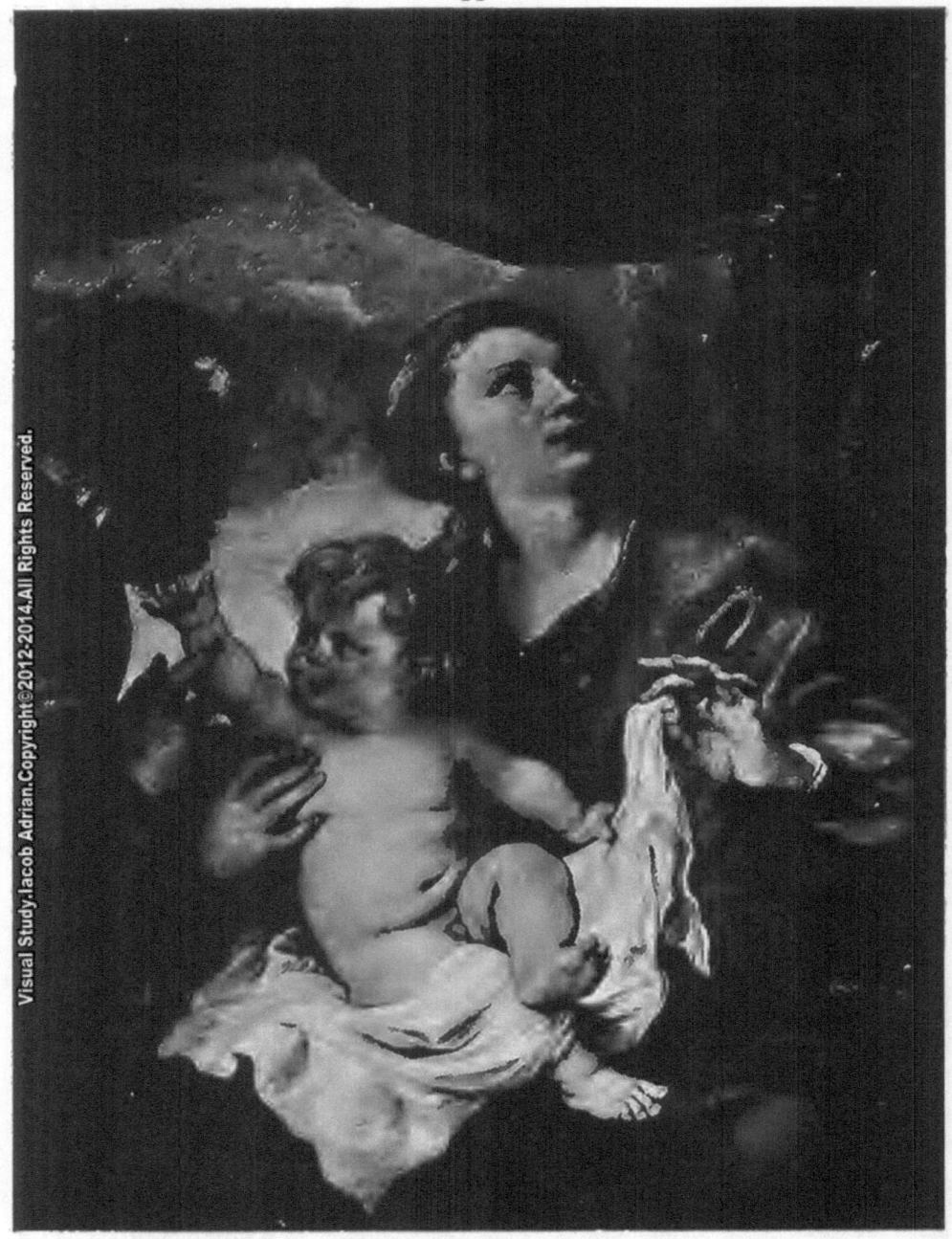

THE HOLY FAMILY
(*Imperial Gallery, Vienna*)

LA SAINTE FAMILLE
(*Galerie impériale, Vienne*)

DIE HEILIGE FAMILIE
(*Wien, Kaiserl. Galerie*)

F. Hanfstaengl. Photo.

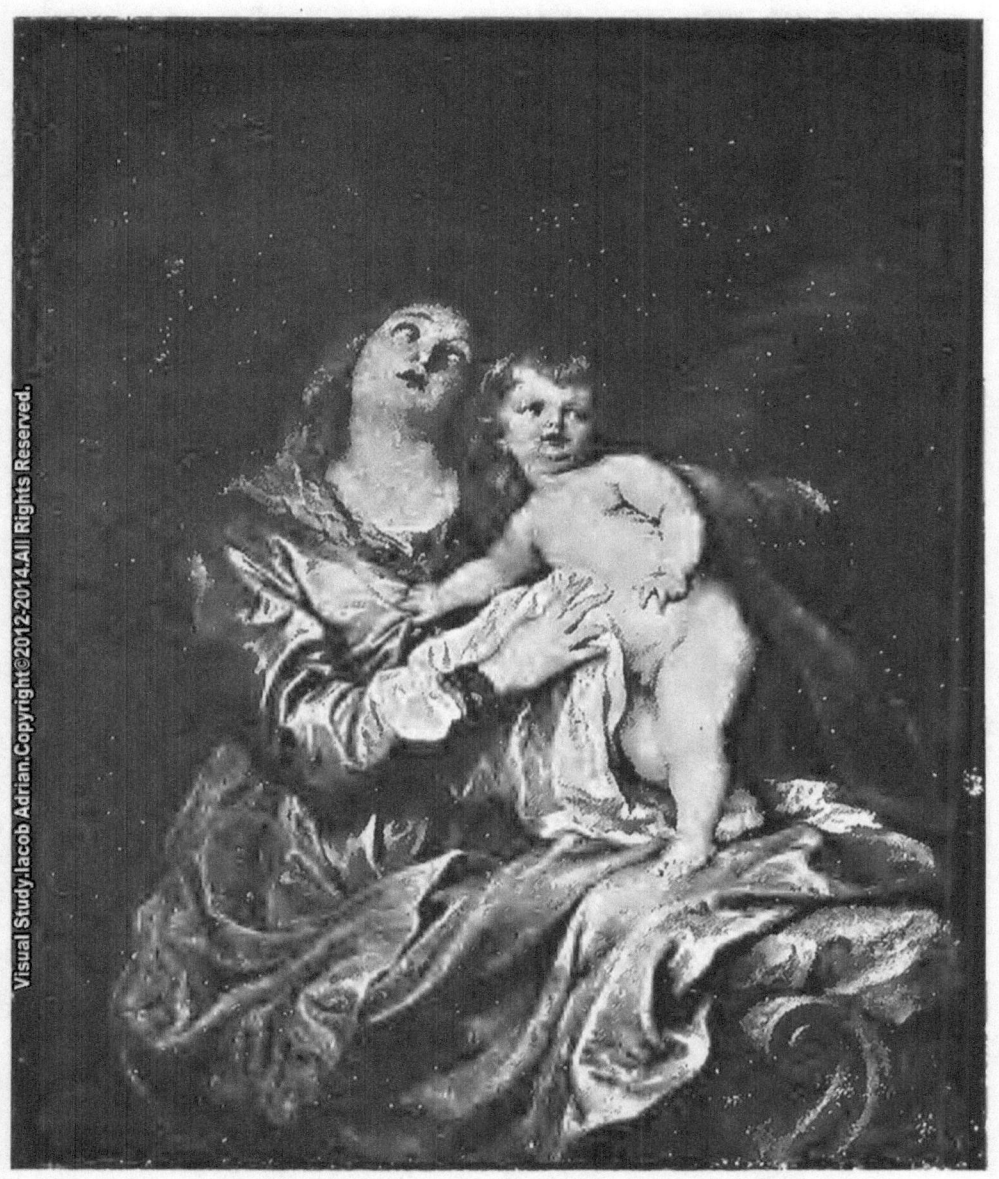

THE VIRGIN AND CHILD
(*Dulwich Gallery*)

LA VIERGE ET L'ENFANT
(*Galerie, Dulwich*)

MADONNA MIT KIND
(*Dulwich, Galerie*)
F. Hanfstaengl, Photo.

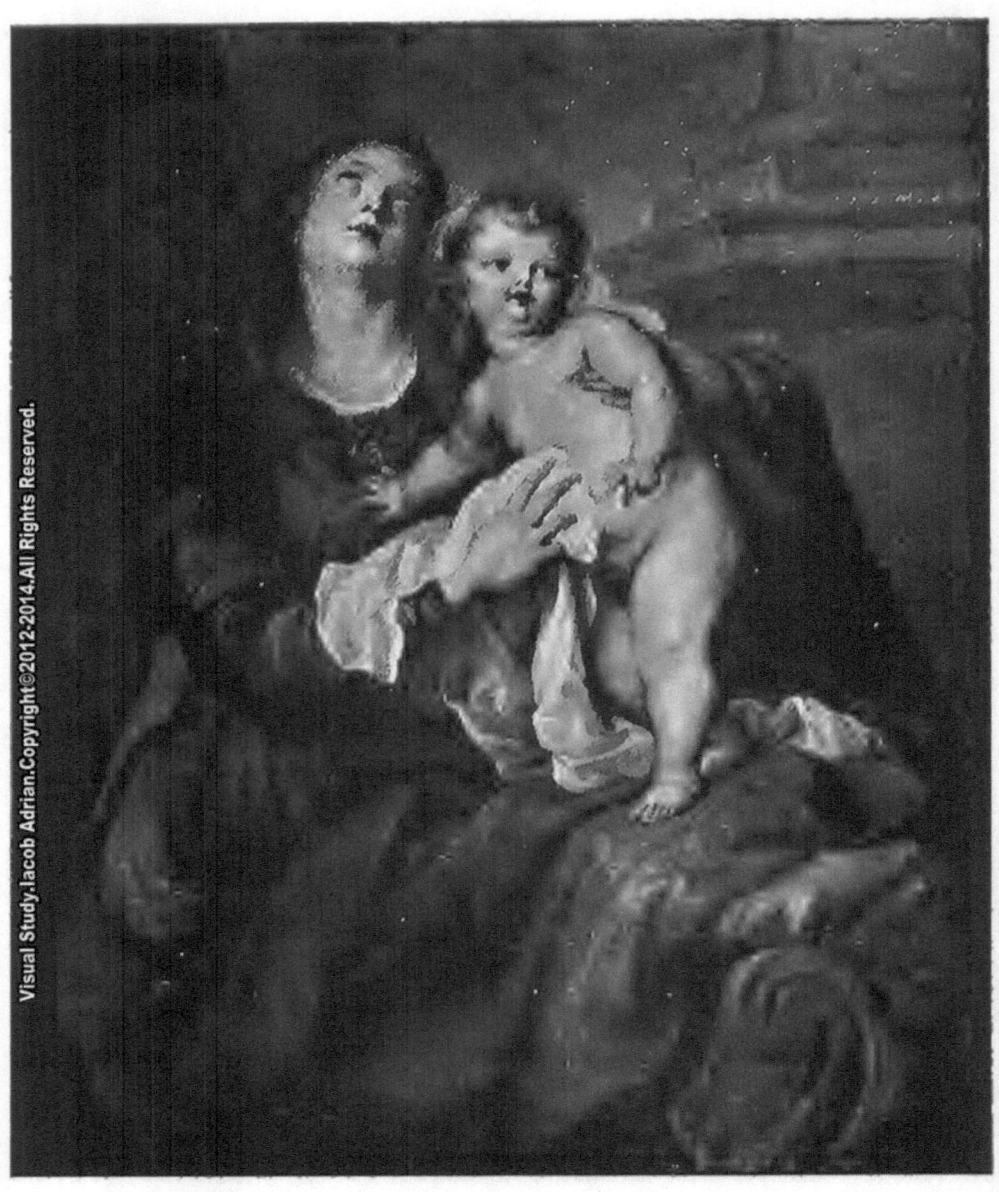

THE VIRGIN AND CHILD   LA VIERGE ET L'ENFANT
(*Liechtenstein Gallery, Vienna*)   (*Galerie Liechtenstein, Vienne*)
MADONNA MIT KIND
(*Wien, Liechtenstein Galerie*)
F. Hanfstaengl, Photo.

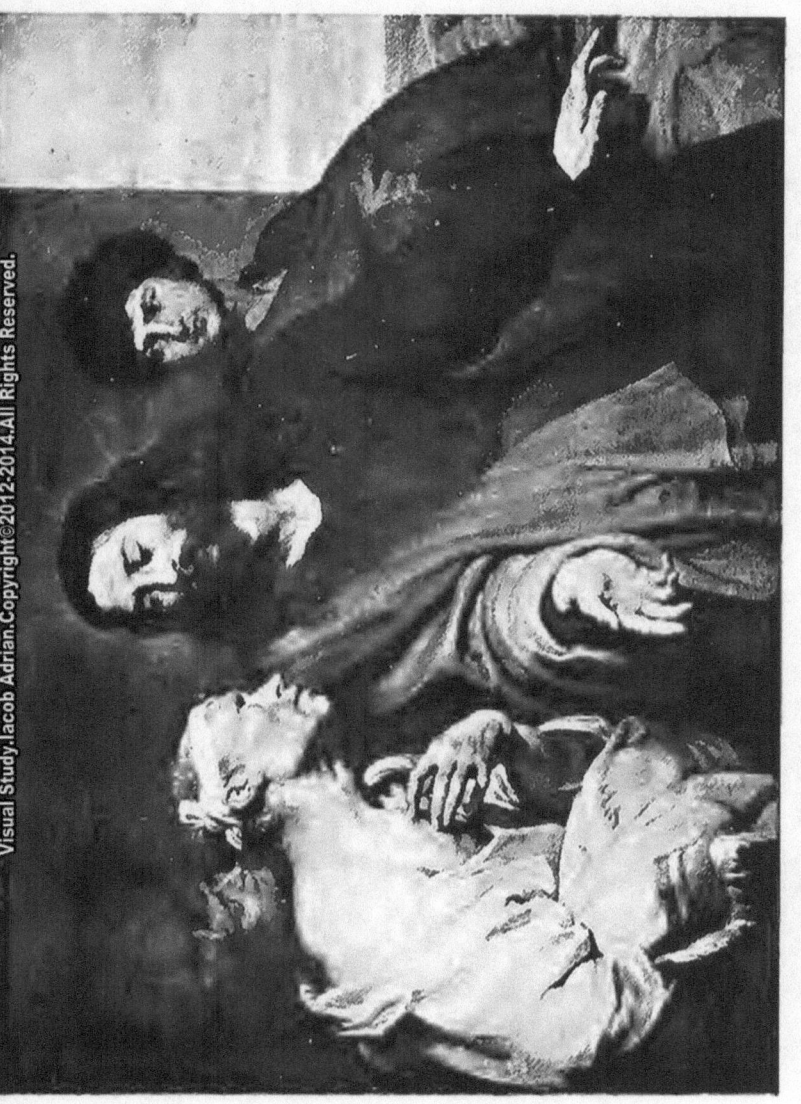

HEALING A SICK WOMAN   LE CHRIST GUÉRISSANT UN MALADE
Buckingham Palace, London)   (Palais Buckingham, Londres)
CHRISTUS, EINE KRANKE FRAU HEILEND
(London, Buckinghampalast)
F. Hanfstaengl, Photo.

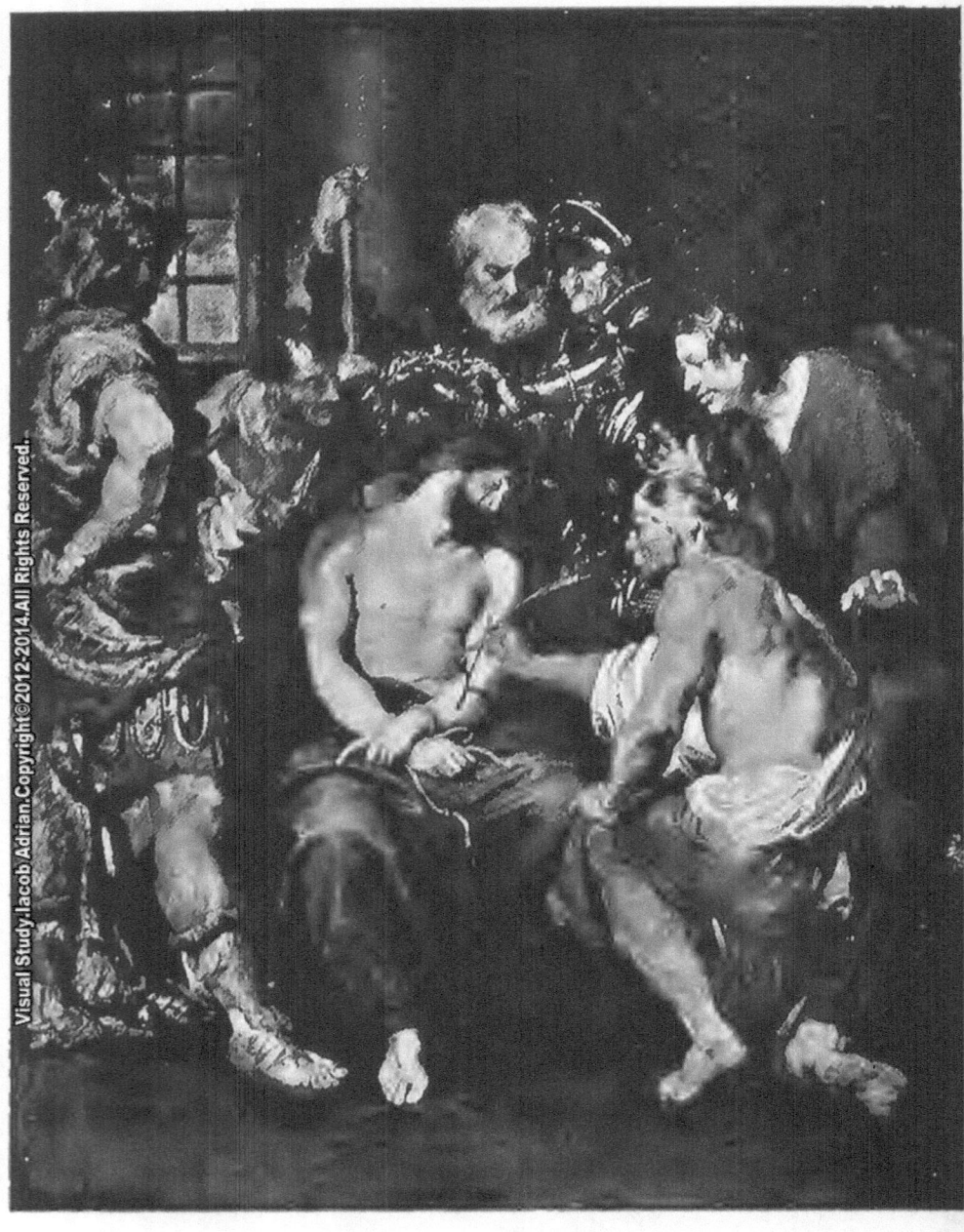

CHRIST MOCKED
(*Royal Gallery, Berlin*)

LE CHRIST OUTRAGÉ ET RAILLÉ
COMME ROI DES JUIFS
(*Musée royal, Berlin*)

VERSPOTTUNG CHRISTI ALS KÖNIG DER JUDEN
(*Berlin, Kgl. Galerie*)
F. Hanfstaengl, Photo.

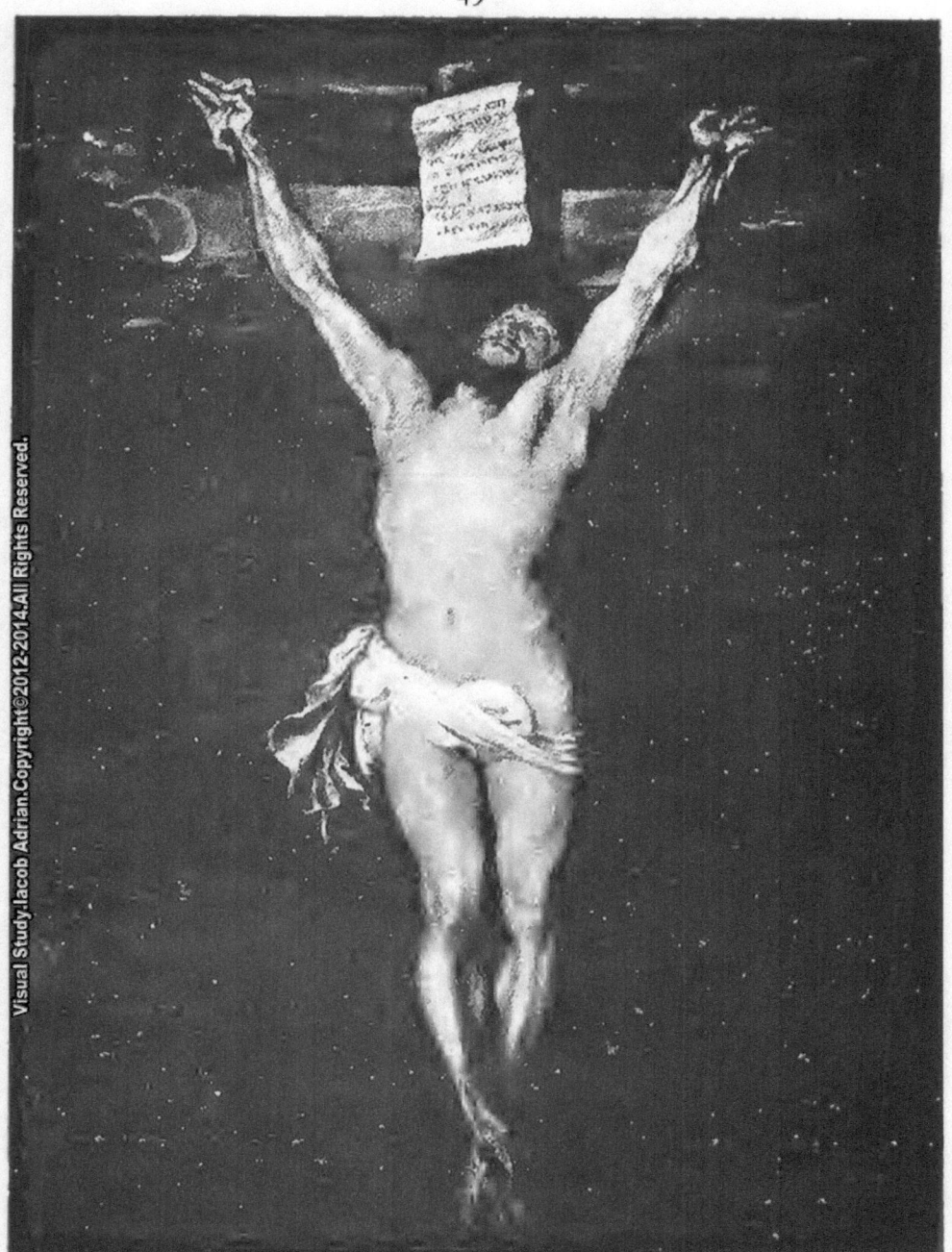

CHRIST ON THE CROSS
(*Academy, Venice*)

LE CHRIST SUR LA CROIX
(*Académie, Venise*)

CHRISTUS AM KREUZ
(*Venedig, Akademie*)
F. Hanfstaengl, Photo.

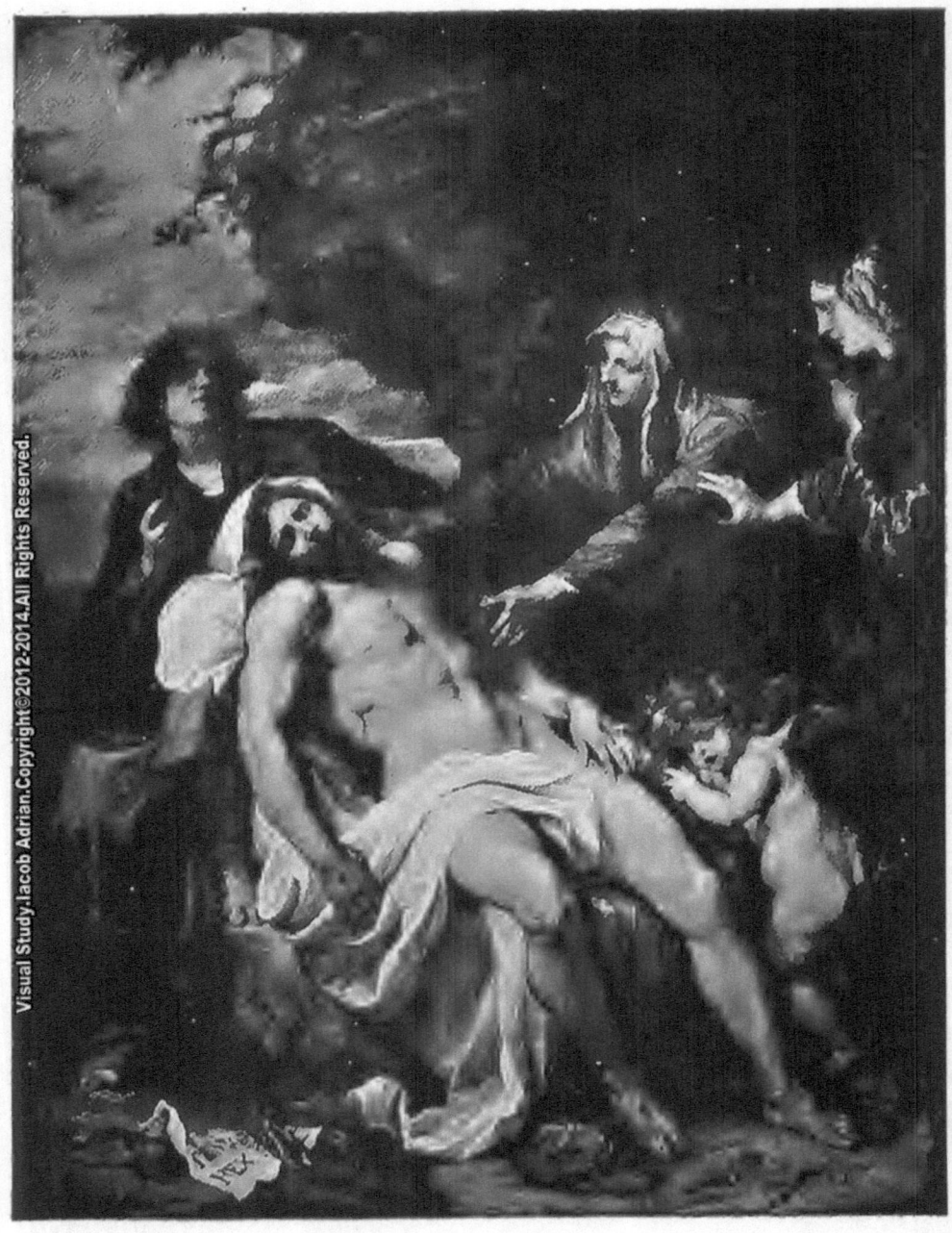

Tiit Mourning for Christ
(Royal Gallery, Berlin)

Le Christ pleuré
(Musée royal, Berlin)

Beweinung Christi
(Berlin, Kgl. Galerie)
F. Hanfstaengl, Photo.

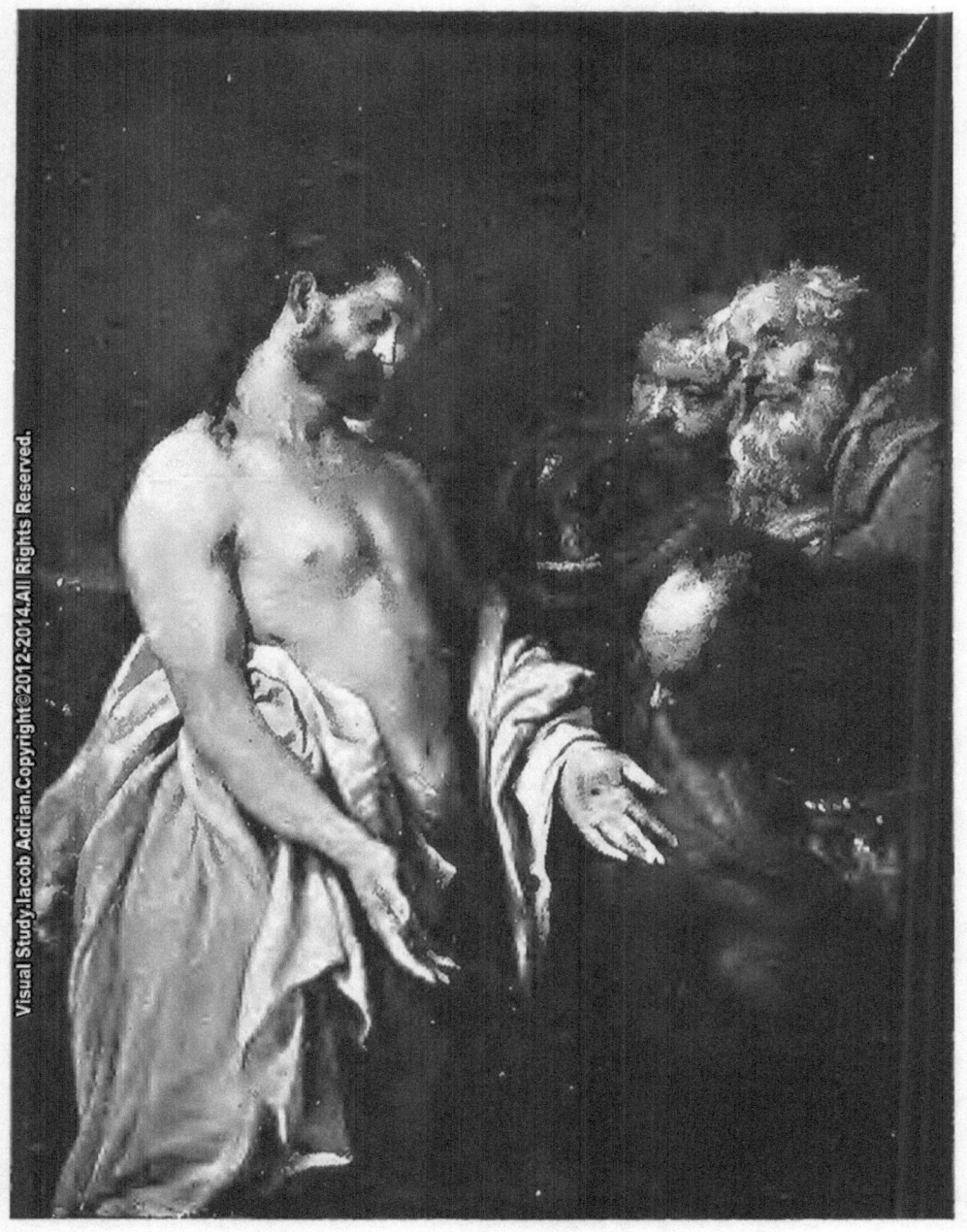

UNBELIEVING THOMAS   L'INCRÉDULITÉ DE SAINT THOMAS
(*The Hermitage, St. Petersburg*) (*L'Ermitage, Saint-Pétersbourg*)
DER UNGLÄUBIGE THOMAS
(*Petersburg, Eremitage*)
F. Hanfstaengl, Photo.

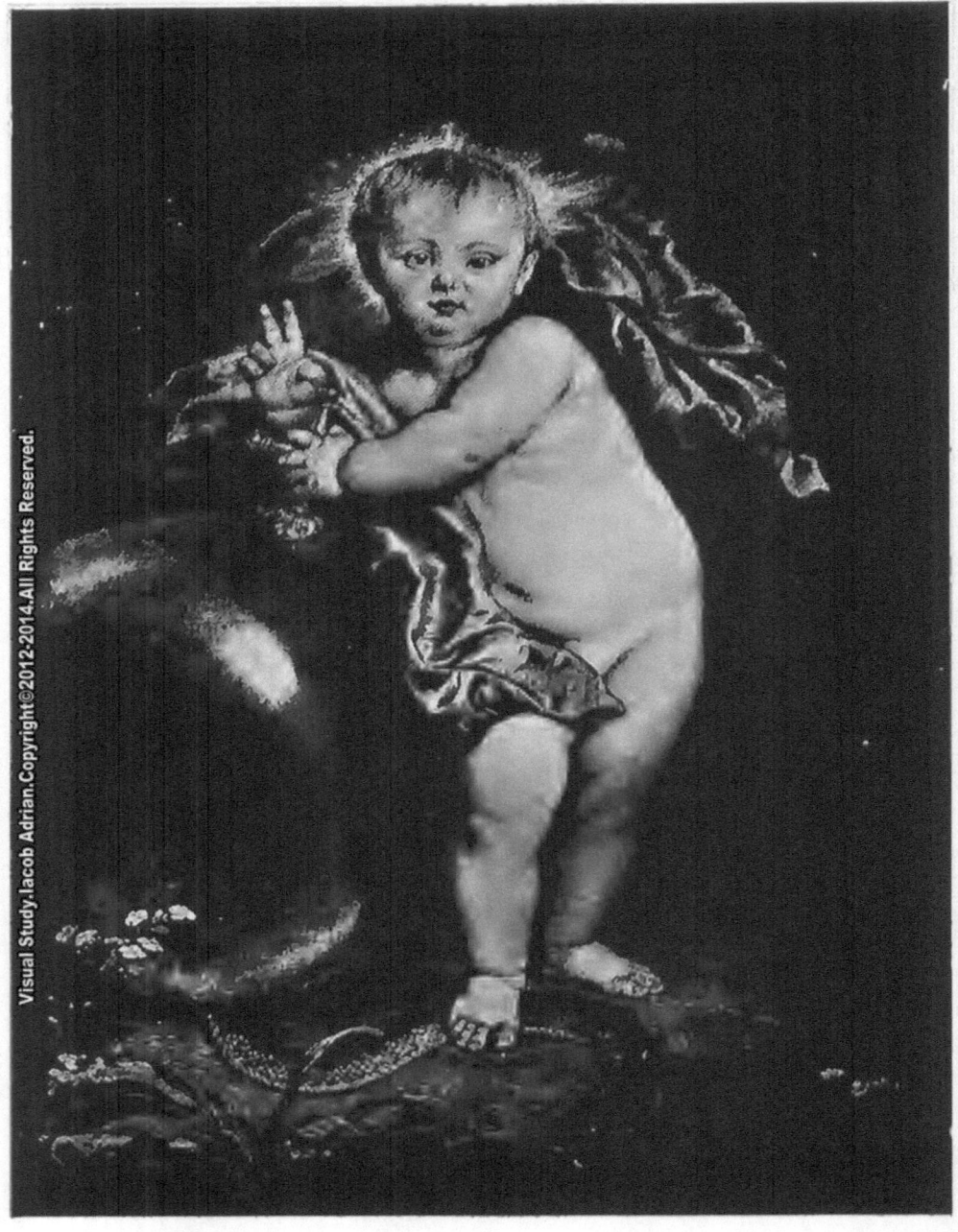

THE BOY JESUS TREADING   L'ENFANT JÉSUS FOULANT AUX PIEDS
ON THE SERPENT   LE SERPENT
(Royal Gallery, Dresden)   (Galerie royale, Dresde)
DER JESUSKNABE, AUF DIE SCHLANGE TRETEND
(Dresden, Kgl. Galerie)
F. Hanfstaengl, Photo.

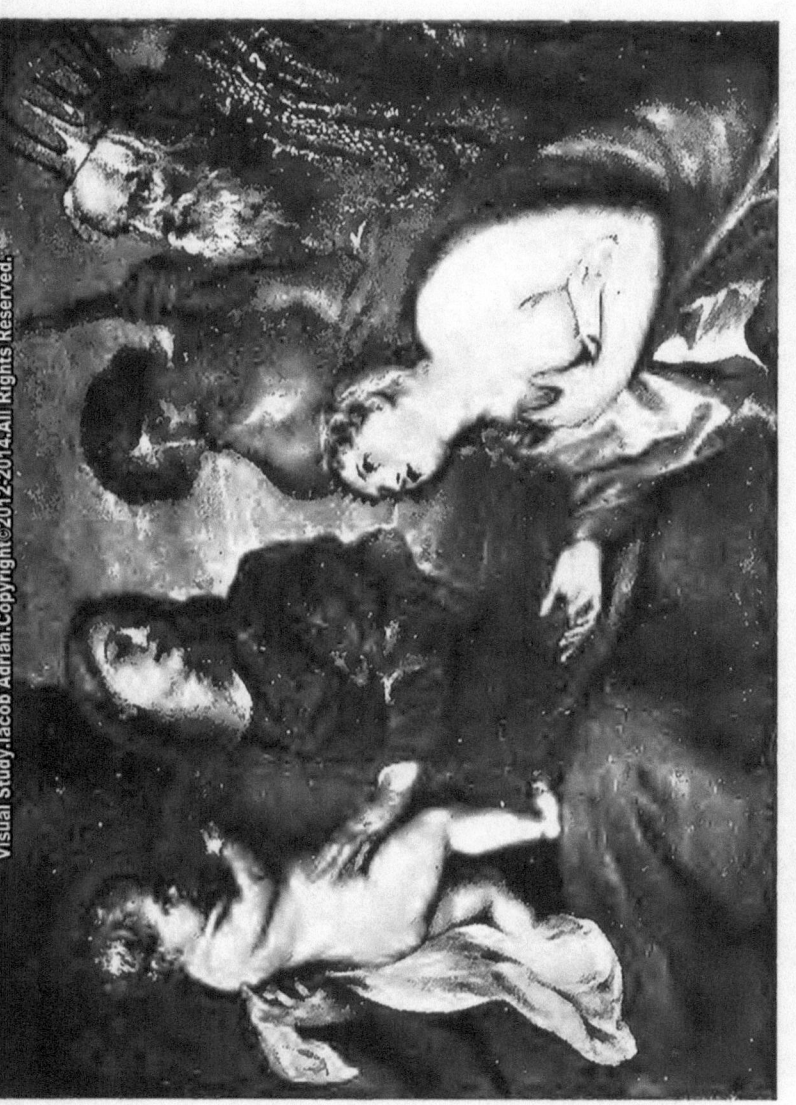

THE REPENTANT SINNERS
(*Royal Gallery, Berlin*)

LES PÉCHEURS REPENTANTS
(*Musée royal, Berlin*)

DIE BUSSFERTIGEN SÜNDER
(*Berlin, Kgl. Galerie*)
F. Hanfstaengl, Photo.

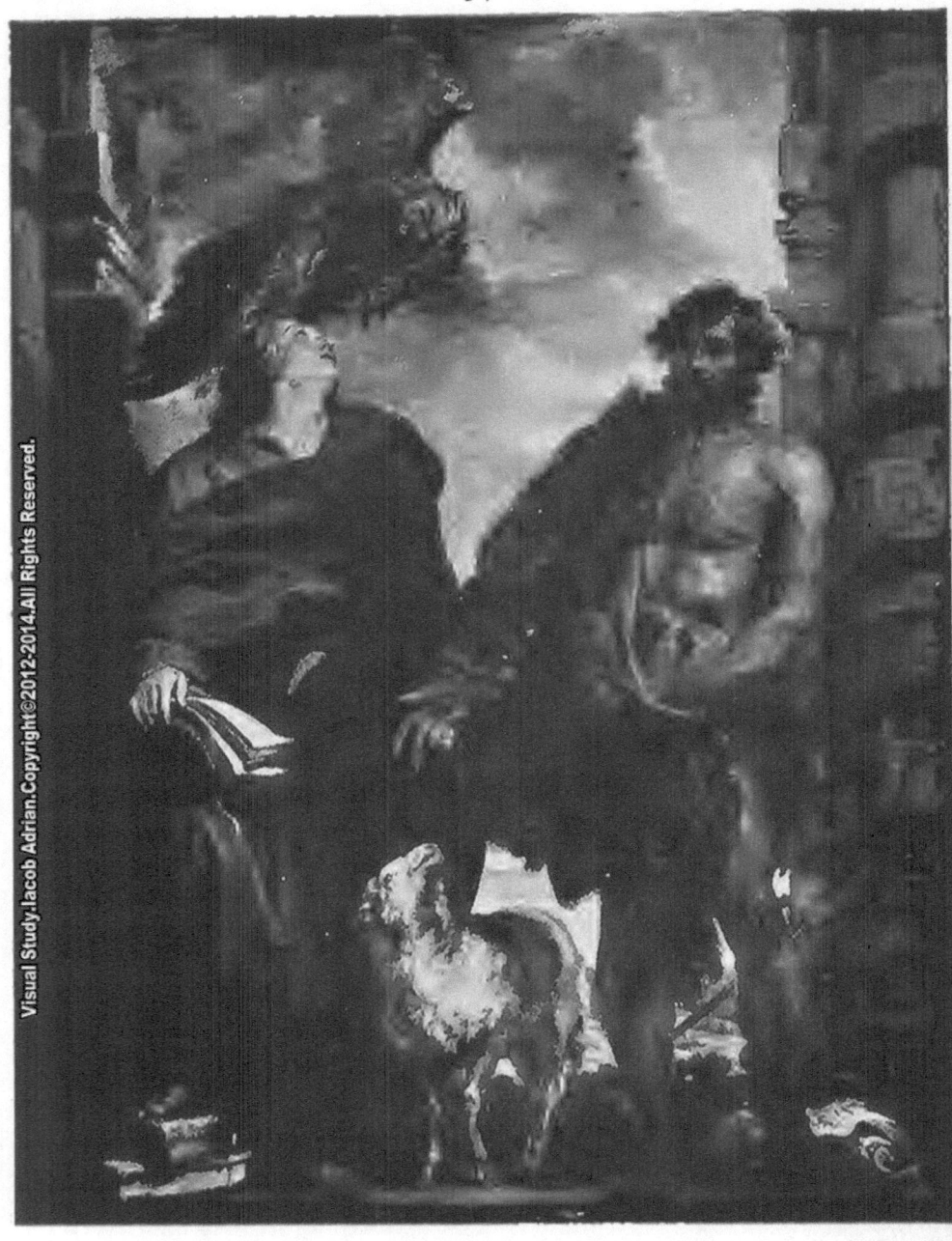

THE TWO JOHNS
(Royal Gallery, Berlin)

LES DEUX JEAN
(Musée royal, Berlin)

DIE BEIDEN JOHANNES
(Berlin, Kgl. Galerie)
F. Hanfstaengl, Photo.

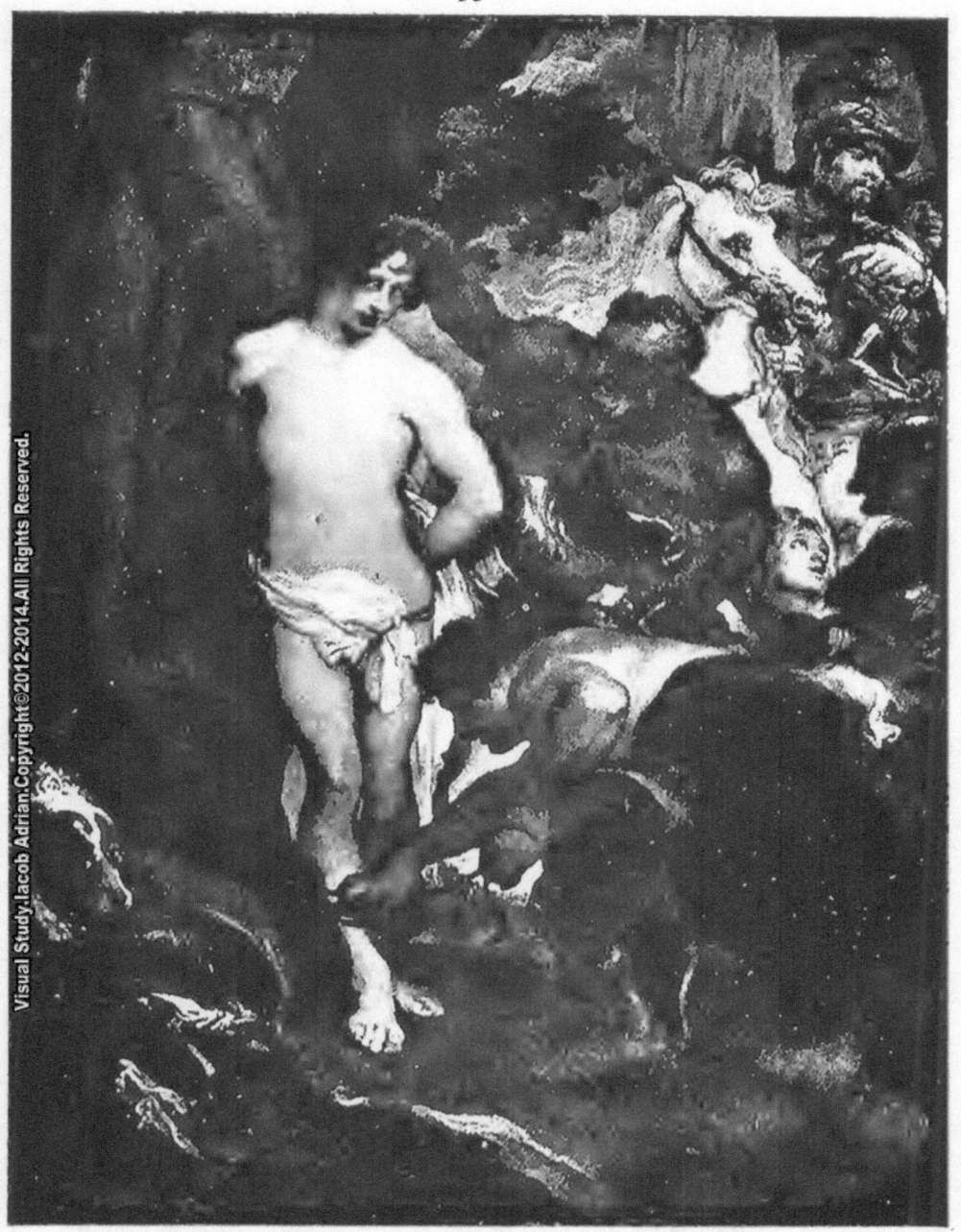

ST. SEBASTIAN
(*Pinakothek, Munich*)

SAINT SÉBASTIEN
(*Pinacothèque, Munich*)

ST. SEBASTIAN
(*München, Pinakothek*)
F. Hanfstaengl, Photo.

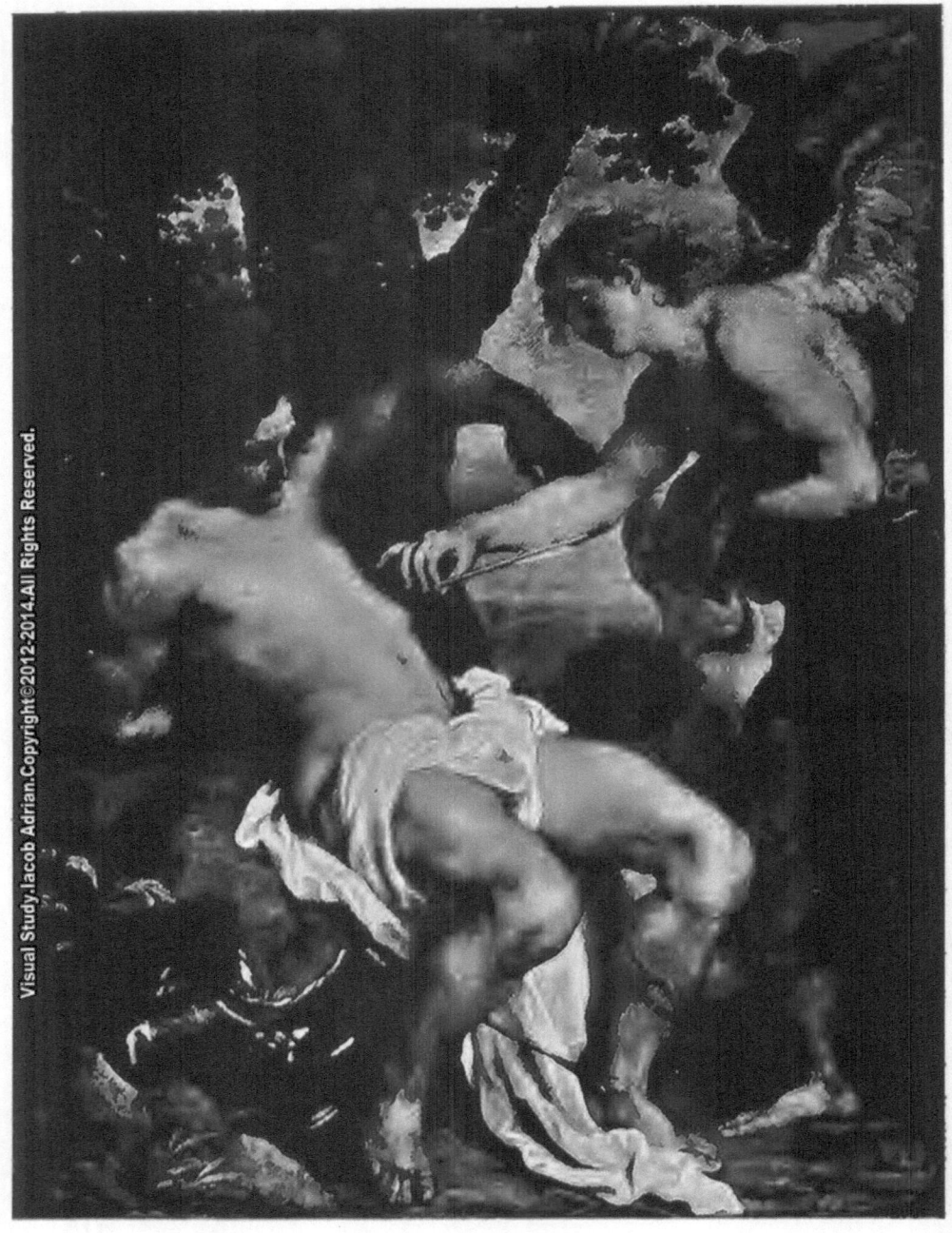

ST. SEBASTIAN   SAINT SÉBASTIEN
(The Hermitage, St. Petersburg)   *(L'Ermitage, Saint-Pétersbourg)*
ST. SEBASTIAN
(Petersburg, Eremitage)
F. Hanfstaengl, Photo.

57

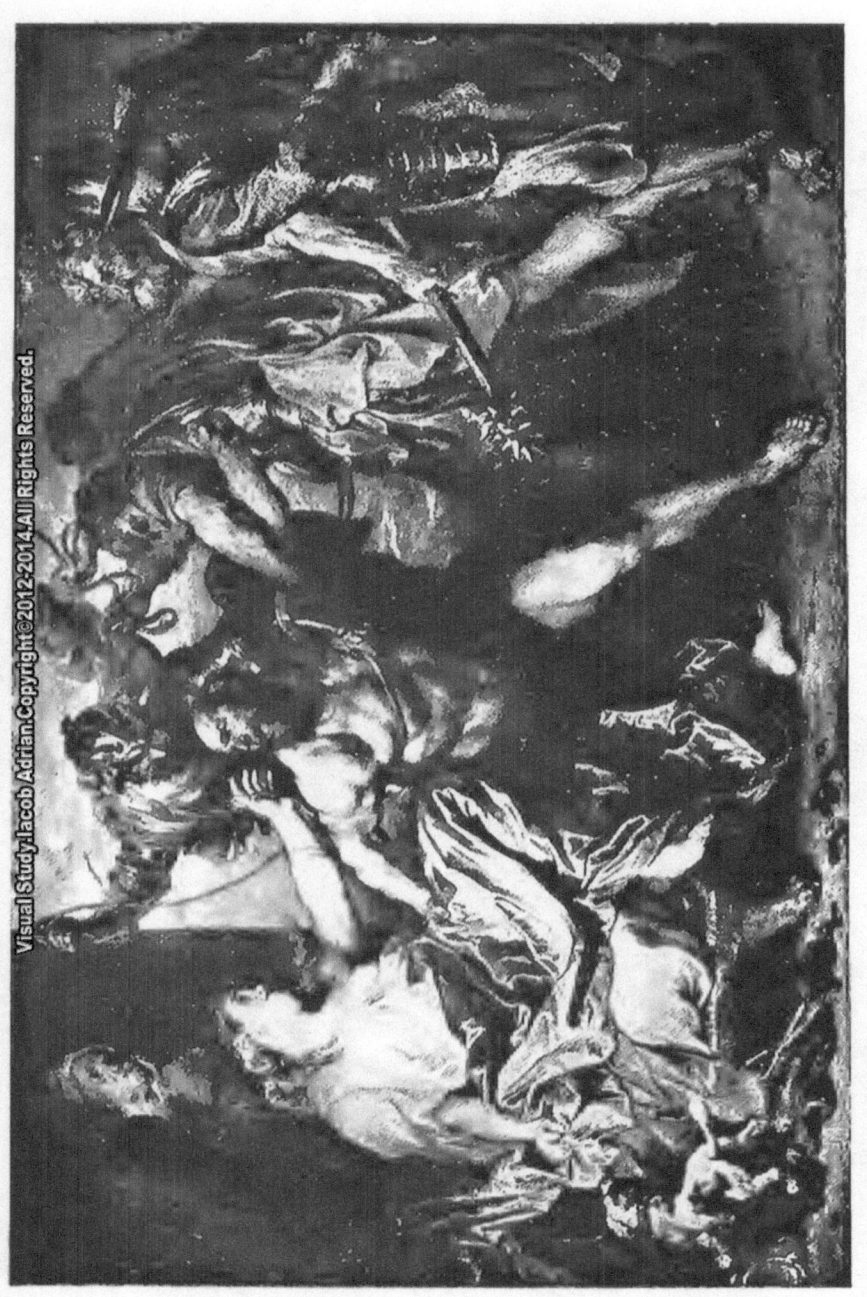

57SAMSON AND DELILAH
(Imperial Gallery, Vienna)

57SAMSON UND DELILA
(Wien, Kaiserl. Galerie)
F. Hanfstaengl, Photo.

57SAMSON ET DALILA
(Galerie impériale, Vienne)

57

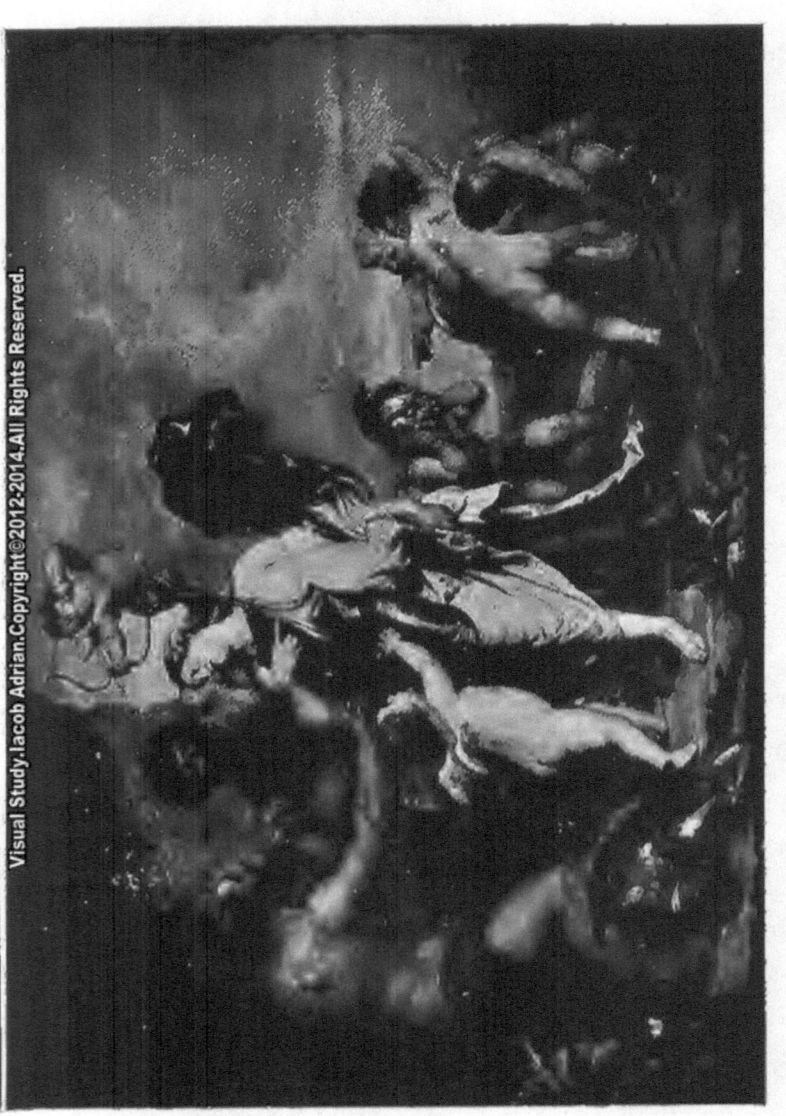

VENUS RECEIVING FROM VULCAN THE   VÉNUS RECEVANT DE VULCAIN LES
WEAPONS FOR ÆNEAS   ARMES POUR ENÉE
(Imperial Gallery, Vienna)   (Galerie impériale, Vienne)
VENUS ERHÄLT VON VULKAN DIE WAFFEN FÜR ÆNEAS
(Wien, Kaiserl. Galerie)
F. Hanfstaengl, Photo.

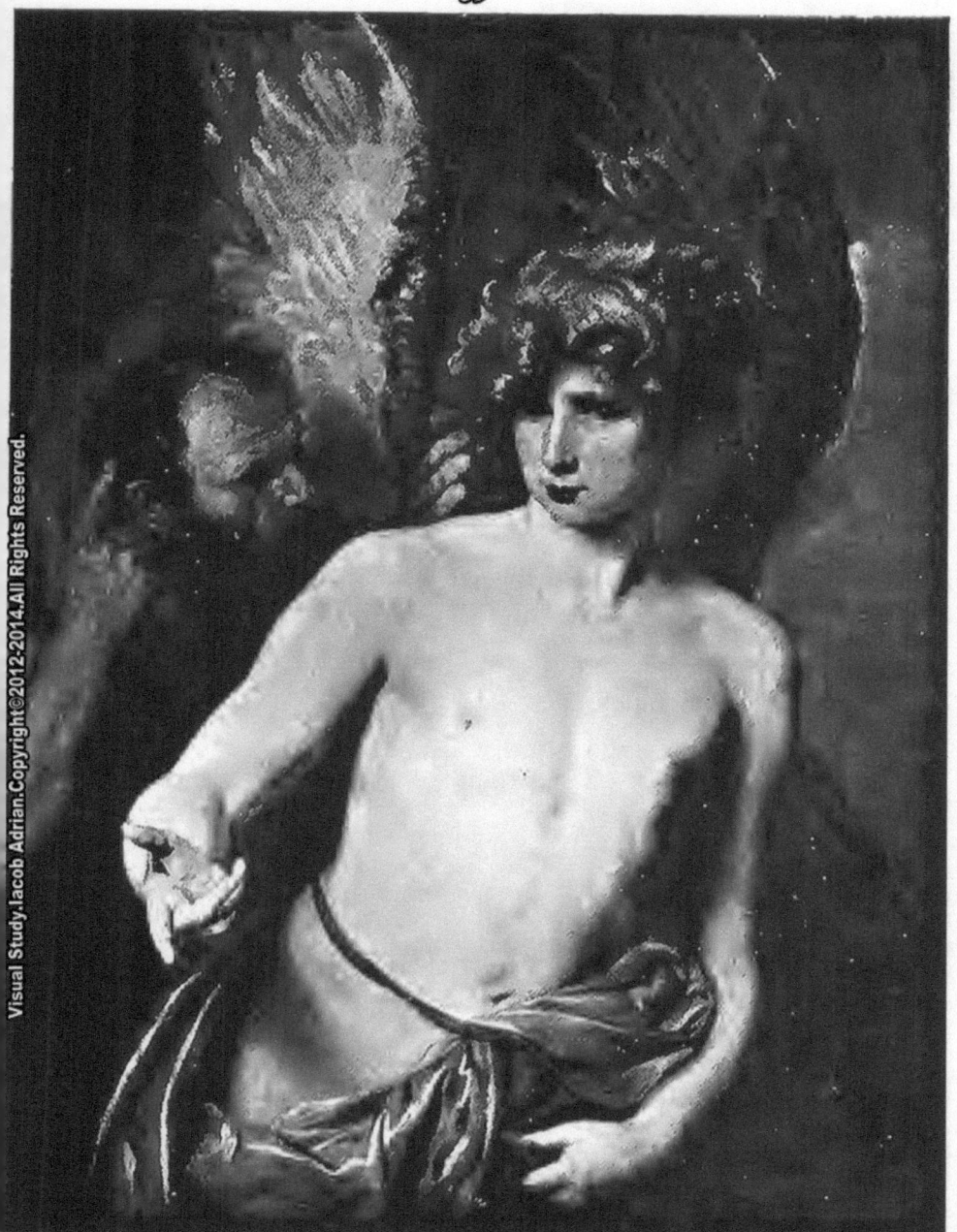

DÆDALUS AND ICARUS   DÉDALE ET ICARE
(Earl Spencer, Althorp)   *(Comte Spencer, Althorp)*

DAEDALUS UND IKARUS
(Althorp, Graf Spencer)
F. Hanfstaengl, Photo.

Bibliographic sources :

The masterpieces of Van Dyck, 1599-1641 : sixty reproductions of photographs from the original paintings by F. Hanfstaengl, affording examples of the different characteristics of the Artist's work (1907)

Author:
Van Dyck, Anthony, 1599-1641
Hanfstaengl, Franz, 1804-1877

Publisher: London : Gowans & Gray, Ltd.

This documentary study use,
combined in various proportions,
elements from the following categories,
forms and subsets :
- fair use
- documentary
- documentary photography
- feature
- journalism
- arts journalism
- visual journalism
- photojournalism
- celebrity photography
in order to :
- employ material as the object of cultural critique ,
- quote to illustrate an argument or point ,
- use material in historical sequence,
providing independent opinion,
using photos, press articles, advertisements,
opinions of fans etc. ...